MIND OVER MICROBES

THE METAPHYSICAL WAY

TRISTAN DC SCHOFIELD

MIND OVER MICROBES:

THE METAPHYSICAL WAY

Printed in the United Kingdom

ISBN: 978 1 5272 6360 4

First Printing, 2020

ACKNOWLEDGMENTS

I would like to express my gratitude to everyone involved in the making and shaping of this book. I would like to thank Laura Wilkinson, for her phenomenal editorial expertise and for her assistance in polishing this manuscript. I would like to thank Sam Alam and Dxer Alam for their creative genius and their magnificent attention to detail regarding the interior and exterior design of the book.

DEDICATION

I dedicate this to Karen Molloy, whose continuous support and inspiration was the rock by which Mind Over Microbes was formulated. Without her the inspiration to write it would have never been conceived. Mother, teacher, best friend and the backbone to all my efforts, words can't express how grateful I am for everything you do.

Contents

ACKNOWLEDGMENTS IV

DEDICATION...V

INTRODUCTION XI

PART I: THE KNOWLEDGE 1

    THE LAW OF ATTRACTION 1

    SCIENTIFIC EXPLANATION OF THE LAW OF
    ATTRACTION 3

    ENERGY FREQUENCY AND VIBRATION.........4

    THOUGHTS....................................5

    THE ANALOGY OF THE RADIO.................6

    THE SYSTEM...................................7

    YOU ARE DESTINED FOR GREATNESS..........8

    PEOPLE COMPLICATE THE ISSUE 8

    THE LAW OF COMPENSATION 9

    THE ANALOGY OF THE GARDEN..............10

    THERE IS NO FIXED PERIOD OF GESTATION .. 12

THE FOUR ESSENTIALS 13

WHAT WE WILL WORK ON 14

IT BEGINS WITH THOUGHT. 15

THE FIVE-STEP PROCESS 16

THE ANALOGY OF THE WRITER 17

DIGGING   DEEPER   INTO   THE   LAW   OF
ATTRACTION 19

THE COLLECTIVE CONSCIOUSNESS 21

THE DOUBLE-SLIT EXPERIMENT 24

HOW TO USE THE LAW OF ATTRACTION. 25

THE WORKINGS OF THE MIND. 26

THOUGHT REVISITED 27

INFINITE INTELLIGENCE 27

THE CONSCIOUS MIND 28

THE SUBCONSCIOUS MIND 29

AUTOSUGGESTION 29

THE CREATIVE IMAGINATION 30

THE SIX BASIC FEARS 30

UNDERSTANDING A VIRUS. 31

A QUICK MESSAGE TO YOU 31

THE PLOT THICKENS 33

POPULATION CONTROL 39

BIOLOGICAL WARFARE 40

CENTRE FOR DISEASE CONTROL 41

ELECTRONIC WARFARE...................... 42

THE MEDIA................................... 44

BACK TO THE LIGHT......................... 45

IT'S ALL PART OF THE DIVINE PLAN 46

PART II: CLEARING THE MIND FOR SUCCESS 49

YOU CAN HAVE, DO, OR BE ANYTHING YOU
WANT 51

TIME AND SPACE 52

THE SIX BASIC FEARS 54

THE UNITY OF CREATION 61

YOU NOW HAVE THE ANSWERS............... 71

SUGGESTION 72

AFFIRMATIONS 75

THE FOUR ESSENTIALS 81

PART III: APPLYING THE KNOWLEDGE TO THE ATTRACTION AND MAINTENANCE OF HEALTH. . 95

ENERGY FREQUENCY AND VIBRATION. 95

THE MEDIA. 97

THE COLLECTIVE CONSCIOUSNESS 99

THE ANALOGY OF THE RADIO. 102

IT BEGINS WITH THOUGHT. 103

THE CONSCIOUS MIND 104

THE SUBCONSCIOUS MIND 105

CREATIVE VISUALISATION. 106

AUTOSUGGESTION 108

BE WHAT YOU WANT TO ATTRACT. 112

PART IV: PRECAUTIONS, PRACTICALITY, AND SUMMARY OF MIND OVER MICROBES. 114

PRECAUTIONS 114

PRACTICALITY 115

SUMMARY OF MIND OVER MICROBES. 117

"To those of whom shall seek. To them... it shall surely find."

INTRODUCTION

This book is for you, the seeker of knowledge and the pursuer of truth. It was written with you in mind with the aim of guarding your mind and protecting your body. It is intended for those who wish to arm themselves with the best defence possible, and for those who will do whatever is necessary to give themselves the knowledge needed for the maintenance of health and the prevention of all other negative circumstances. It is for the men and women who will act on the teachings of this book in pure faith while casting all worries and doubts aside. For such people, this book will most definitely work. It will provide the reader with a defence unlike no other. It will guard you mentally and physically by arming you with the mindset necessary to protect you from a multitude of diseases and various other negative influences. If you understand the principles outlined in this book, and if you apply them, you will create for yourself a safety haven; you will forge the walls of a heavenly mansion thus guarding your mind and, ultimately, protecting your body.

The book was written for—but is not limited to—the outbreak of coronavirus. Since the virus made its first appearance, it has gripped the attention of the world and has instilled fear in the minds of the many who shiver at the thought of potentially contracting the disease. The prospect of being quarantined and treated like animals is a scary one indeed, and in times like this, measures need to be taken to protect yourself from succumbing to this maltreatment. During a quarantine, you essentially have no rights and are treated as though you are an infected prisoner.

And so, I write this book to prevent the contraction of the disease, to prevent being quarantined, and to protect you in all walks of life. This book will teach nothing that has not been taught throughout the centuries; the book will not teach anything that a good amount of the world does not already know. But what it will do is organize that information and present it to you in a quick, easy, and practical way for you to apply in your own life, and, in relation to, a multitude of diseases. It will present you with the necessary knowledge of the virus, its attributes, and provide you with the precautions needed to make use of the defence which will be taught. The book will cover topics such as the law of attraction, the law of compensation, the conscious mind, the subconscious mind, autosuggestion, and the collective consciousness. I will also be speaking about a sinister hidden plot that exists right here on earth.

I have studied the principles outlined with dedication and precision for over a decade. I have used these principles in my own life and have benefited astronomically from them, and you will, too. I have made this book as short as I could to give you an easy read and to keep out all non-essential information. The work that follows derives from many years of research and study and is the result of a combination of metaphysics and psychology. I have combined philosophy and science together because the two go hand in hand; for one deals with the cause of things, whilst the other studies, and deals with, its effect. The scientific principles and philosophies contained herein are derived from the teachings of some of the world's greatest minds.

Napoleon Hill, Nikola Tesla, Wallace D Wattles, Stuart Wilde, Bob Proctor, Earnest Holmes, Earl Nightingale, Alan Watts, Dr Joseph Murphy, Norman Vincent Peale, Esther Hicks, Allan and Barbara Pease, James Allen, Dr Joe Dispenza, Bentinho Massaro, Rhonda Byrne, David Icke, Eckhart Tolle and Florence Scovel Shinn.

I ask with humility that you use the principles in this book in full faith and you do exactly what the book tells you to do. In an instance such as a pandemic, it would be detrimental not to. When a pandemic of this magnitude occurs, you have but one of two options; you can leave the situation in the hands of chance, while you wait, in a state of fear and hope for the best, or you can take responsibility for the situation and induce a positive mental attitude as you embody the emotion of faith to create the reality that you want. The latter, of course, being the best option by far.

In making use of the principles, you have nothing to lose but everything to gain. The principles described are flawless; they will work. They are based on universal laws, and universal laws do not err. The working of the principles depends only on your willingness to work them. I have no doubt you will make use of the knowledge herein, for if that was not the case, the book would have never ended up in your hands. You will soon discover that the universe operates through law and order; it cannot, and never does, operate through disorder or chance. So, the very fact that you are holding this book, is proof enough that you were destined to read it, benefit from it, and protect yourself from the circumstances of life which may seem outside of your control. Not only will this book protect you from a virus, but it will also protect you from a wide array of negative circumstances. That is, if you so desire such protection.

The book will work in four parts. First, I am going to present to you all the information and knowledge that you need. Second, we are going to work on clearing the mind in order to make use of the knowledge. Third, we are going to apply the knowledge we have learned and tie the knowledge to the maintenance of health. And fourth, I will apply some precautions, some practicality, and a summary.

Part I will be replicated slightly in Part III, however, this time it will be in relation to the application of preventing disease and maintaining health, but this replication was done with purpose. The reason for doing so was twofold. Firstly, because I want you to grasp the concepts outlined for what they actually are, as I feel it would be difficult to understand them if we tied them to preventing a disease right off the bat. The concepts are much easier to internalise on their own to start with. And secondly, because repetition is key. Studies suggest that learning is more effective with systematic repetition. So, by internalising and digesting the principles first, then later applying the principles to their intended purpose, it will provide you with a far better understanding of them and it will ultimately have a much greater impact for you.

Follow through with persistence, with full faith, and this book will do you wonders. Whatever your reason for holding this book, it was written with you in mind and with the goal to keep you protected. I will show you the door, but it is you who must walk through it. I will be here with you, every step of the way.

PART I: THE KNOWLEDGE

THE LAW OF ATTRACTION

The law of attraction is a phenomenon that has been philosophized and mentioned throughout the ages. Philosophers have observed this phenomenon and it has been widely written about by all the great thinkers of the past. It is still spoken about by the great thinkers of the present, and it will be spoken about by the thinkers of the future. Sadly, the general population have been kept in the dark and remain unaware of the phenomenon, and the few who have been lucky enough to be introduced to it, simply don't understand it, so it generally gets misunderstood and quite often disregarded due to the misunderstanding.

It has been taught in the Bible. It has been taught in the Qur'an. Buddhists have preached it for thousands of years, and it is referenced time and time again in the Torah. All religions have acknowledged this truth but they do so indirectly, and they tend to reference the phenomenon metaphorically, to leave it open to interpretation. Most men and women who read religious scriptures don't analyse its metaphorical method of expression and the men and women reading usually take what is being read too literally. Which is unfortunate because they overlook the metaphorical meaning, and so they ultimately miss the message. Although it has been referenced time and time again throughout our existence, it is only until recently that people are waking up to the phenomenon. The misunderstanding is slowly fading away and humanity is finally getting to grips with it.

Before the movie 'The Secret' by Rhonda Byrne was released in 2006, it remained relatively unknown. But in light of the film, it opened the door of awareness to millions of people around the world and she gave them a peek into the workings of the great universal law. This peek into the universal law has taken the world by storm and it has gripped the attention of many by teaching its principles in a simple, but effective way. Now more and more people are becoming aware and hearing about one of the greatest—if not the greatest—discoveries known to man.

The law of attraction is a universal law; it operates on a universal scale and it never fails to do so. The universe operates according to law and order, never by disorder and chance. Just like the law of polarity, the law of cause and effect, the law of correspondence, and so on, the law of attraction is a law of the universe and it is one of the 12 universal laws that we are aware of. It always works, it never fails. Because, in the universe, there is a power. An intelligence. This intelligence follows night with day and autumn with winter. It causes the leaves to fall in response to gravity and it keeps the earth spinning in perpetual motion. Autumn will never forget to arrive, and gravity will always drop the leaf. The sun doesn't forget to rise because the earth will never forget to spin. The universe doesn't struggle to maintain its laws. But it would struggle to break them. The law of attraction always works, it never fails, and it never can. It's a mathematical impossibility. The basic premise of the law of attraction is that like attracts like. Quite simply, if you think in positive terms, you get positive results; if you think in negative terms, you get negative results. For like causes will always produce like effects. What you think, feel, and believe, you will receive.

"The universe operates by using law and order. It never operates and can never operate by disorder or chance."

SCIENTIFIC EXPLANATION OF THE LAW OF ATTRACTION

The reticular activating system (RAS) is located in the brain stem and it connects to various other parts of the brain. The RAS filters incoming sensory information and decides what information will make it into your conscious awareness. Whatever you see, hear, taste or touch passes through the RAS. Since your brain picks up millions of bits of information every second, and since we can only register consciously about two thousand bits, the RAS filters out the bits that are not relevant to you at the time. The RAS is like a GPS; you tap into it the things of relevance and it will point out to you anything which is linked to that thing while filtering out all the non-essentials. You could be in a busy shopping centre and hear your name, for example. There are many other noises going on around you but it prioritises anything of relevance and filters out all the non-essential sounds; your RAS picks up the essential sound automatically and you then respond by looking around in an attempt to work out who said it. Or another example is that you buy a new car, let's say a blue BMW for instance. Suddenly, everyone has one; you see your car everywhere you go. Not because they have manufactured more blue BMW's since you bought yours, but because the car is now associated with you and it has relevance. And so, your RAS alerts you to it. The cars were always there before you got yours, but because of a lack of association, your RAS didn't alert your attention to them. If you recently developed the desire to start yoga, you will suddenly begin to see yoga class advertisements, or you will hear yoga being mentioned in a conversation. Due to your newly found interest in yoga, you tap that information into the GPS that is the reticular activating system, and so it commences on routing relevant associations. The RAS is likened to a heat-seeking missile that seeks out only its associated target. Have you ever thought of somebody that you haven't heard from in a long time? Then, for some strange reason, this person calls you, or you bump into them, or they get mentioned by someone else? That's your RAS at work and that is, the law of attraction.

"What you think about, you bring about."

– Bob Proctor

ENERGY FREQUENCY AND VIBRATION

If you wish to understand the law of attraction and how to use it, you need to understand that the universe—and everything in the universe—consists of energy, frequency, and vibration. All matter is merely energy condensed and vibrating to a specific frequency. Physicists studying string theory will tell you that if we use a microscope to zoom into the particle of an object, down to atomic level and then even further down to sub-atomic level, the seemingly solid, seemingly still particle is actually nothing more than a vibrating string of energy.

"If you wish to understand the universe think in terms of energy frequency and vibration."

-Nikola Tesla

THOUGHTS

The same applies to your thoughts. Thoughts are things. And they are very real. Thoughts are intangible impulses of energy and they, too, vibrate to a specific frequency. Being intangible, they are mistakenly regarded as something which is not real. People have been taught to disregard the things which they cannot physically observe with their senses, but we cannot observe gravity and that is intangible—it does not mean it doesn't exist. Since we observe the leaf fall from the tree, and since we can see the effect of the fallen leaf, we do not fail to accept that there is a cause, which we call gravity. However, when it comes to thought, we don't acknowledge that they, too, are a cause; a cause which is also intangible. The thought caused you to choose your phone. Your thoughts caused you to buy this book. Just because we cannot see something, it doesn't mean it is not real, and it doesn't mean it is not there.

"Ideas are more real than the physical brain in which the thoughts have been housed, for they have the ability to live on, even when the brain that housed them has long turned to dust."

-Napoleon Hill

THE ANALOGY OF THE RADIO

Thoughts are impulses of energy, the purest form of energy there is, they vibrate just like everything else and they operate on a frequency. Radio operates on a frequency, and to change the channel, you tune into the frequency of the channel you want to listen to. Thoughts operate in the same way, and you must tune into the frequency of the reality you want to experience. Have you ever asked yourself, what does complete silence sound like? If not, I have a task for you. Remove yourself from all surrounding sound. Find a place where there is absolutely no noise. Preferably in bed at night, but anywhere with no noise will do. Now, just listen. What does complete silence sound like? We will never know. Do you hear that ringing in your ears? That's the frequency that you're on. In changing our thought patterns, we can even hear the pitch of the frequency change because when you change your thoughts, after a while, your feelings change, and the result is a change in the pitch of the ringing in your ears.

To manifest a desire into your life, whatever it may be, you must tune your thoughts into the frequency of that desire and align your thoughts with that reality. In metaphysical terms, the universe is infinite and so all potentialities, and all realities you could possibly imagine exists for you; in intangible form, simultaneously. Our reality is very much like a radio that has infinite channels, and you can tune into any channel you want; you can experience any reality which you desire. But first, you must learn how to turn the dial. We all turn the dial subconsciously, but we want to learn how to turn it consciously and with purpose. Because, unless you have an uncanny positive mental attitude by default, and unless your mind is naturally immune to outside influence, it would do you no favours to leave the dial turning on autopilot.

> *"Looking for consciousness in the brain is like looking in a radio for the announcer. Our brains do not contain consciousness, they tune into it."*
>
> – Nassim Harrmein

THE SYSTEM

We live in a system which has been designed to keep you thinking about the things which you don't want. The system thrives off pessimism, gossip, problems, and negative emotions. Pessimistic people, gossiping about 'problems' because of their negative emotions. The system is designed to keep people in that frequency. It is purposely designed to keep our thoughts vibrating on the frequency of fear, doubt, and worry. It's quite rare that you see optimistic people, constructively speaking about solutions using positive emotions. But when you do, they are usually the people who have all the things that they want. These kinds of people make up about 20% of the earth's population, and so it's no wonder why 20% of the earth's population earns around 80% of the earth's wealth. Those who don't take control of their own mind and guard themselves against negative outside influences generally end up working for those who do.

> *"People fall out of your life as your frequency rises. Let them go, that's a part of your frequency rising."*

YOU ARE DESTINED FOR GREATNESS

The fact you are reading this book tells me you belong in the twenty per cent group. Because it proves you desire to take control of your life, and you earnestly seek the knowledge needed to protect yourself from the negative influences of the world. In reading this book, you are asking for life to yield to you all the positive experiences that you wish to experience, and with that determination, the law of attraction will bring to you those experiences; which you truly deserve.

> *"Whatever the mind can conceive and believe, the mind can achieve."*
>
> *– Napoleon Hill*

PEOPLE COMPLICATE THE ISSUE

The law of attraction is a very simple law and it is often made to be more complicated than it needs to be. For some strange reason, mainly a lack of understanding, people always seem to complicate the issue, and I will explain why. When people attempt to put the law of attraction into conscious use, they begin with a sense of enthusiasm and they tend to start out in excitement about the possibilities connected with making use of the law.

With their newfound excitement, they attempt to practice the power of positive thinking. And then they begin to practice the art of creative visualisation. They start to build on their excitement and positivity and so, they begin to tip the balance. They begin to shift their mind from a negative, pessimistic view to a positive, optimistic one. Everything seems to be going well. But then, something happens. They look around and because they don't see the results that they want right away, because the picture that they have visualised in their minds hasn't shown up yet—the health, the car, the house, the money, the relationship—they become disheartened. And so, their thought pattern shifts right back to the negative vibration as a result. If you think in negative terms, you will get negative results. The disappointment is a form of negativity and so the negative circumstances persist. If enthusiasm is a form of positivity, then why didn't they achieve the positive results? Because there is a time delay.

"According to your faith be it done unto you."

- Matthew [9:29]

THE LAW OF COMPENSATION

Most people who attempt to consciously make use of the law of attraction don't understand the time delay between manifestations. They don't understand another universal law, one which is a necessity to understand when making use of the law of attraction successfully. This law which operates in conjunction with the law of attraction is just as important but is rarely even spoken about. And so those attempting to manifest health, wealth, and relationships rarely succeed because they don't seem to understand the law of compensation. This law is where the old saying comes from, 'you reap what you sew'. Most people have heard this saying but very few actually understand the truth behind it or are aware that it is a universal law. When those attempting to consciously make use of the law of attraction fail, it's because they don't realise that there is a season for sewing and a season for reaping.

"As you sew, so shall you reap."

THE ANALOGY OF THE GARDEN

When a farmer wants a carrot, he sews the carrot seed. But he does not reap the carrot for ninety days because there is a gestation period. During the gestation period, the farmer will nurture his crop while ensuring it has an ample amount of water and sunlight; but he certainly doesn't help it grow by feeding it poison. When it comes to manifesting a thought form into a physical reality, there is a gestation period also and in its period of gestation, negative thoughts such as doubt or disbelief are likened to feeding the seed of your desire poison. When you plant the seed of desire, you must fertilize that seed constantly. You must nurture the seed, care for it, and understand that the season you plant the seed is not the season you will reap the result.

If you think of your mind as being like a garden. You will see that the method of turning an intangible desire into a tangible reality is the same as the method by which you would turn a tiny seed into a carrot. When the farmer grows a carrot, he first clears the soil in which the carrot will germinate. He then clears out the weeds and he cultivates the land to ensure that the soil is as rich and as receptive as possible. Next, he plants the seed. Once the seed has been planted, he continues to nurture the seed by looking after the plot of land. He makes sure the plot has adequate sunlight and is watered regularly. In the meantime, he waits with a positive expectation that the seed will eventually spring from the ground in the form of a carrot. He waits patiently because he understands the carrots period of gestation. He understands the rules for nurturing the plot of land, and so he feels positive and expectant that he will get a positive result. He doesn't ever doubt the process, he never goes through moments of unbelief and his faith never wavers. For he knows that you reap what you sew and if one sews the seed of carrot, and if one abides by the rules of caring for the seed's growth, then the universe can't help but ensure that he reaps a carrot. The universe can never give him a potato in its place, and it never will because the universe operates according to law and order; it never operates by disorder or chance. And like causes will always produce like effects. Each seed vibrates to its own frequency and when planted, each seed attracts to it the energy of the same frequency; it attracts the energy of its kind which, in turn, will produce the circumstance aligned to its vibrational match. You cannot plant a potato seed and expect a carrot and you cannot plant a carrot seed and expect a potato.

The transmuting of thought into a physical actuality can be likened to the analogy of the garden. And the same laws which govern the germination of a vegetable applies to the germination of desire into a physical actuality. The laws are universal. The gestation period of a human being is nine months. The season you reap the baby is not the same season which you sew the seed. This is where those who wish to consciously make use of the law of attraction make the mistake of not understanding the law of compensation. We understand it in the physical world, but very few understand it and use it in the spiritual world, although its operation there is just as undeviating.

"Dreams are the seedlings of reality."

– Napoleon Hill

THERE IS NO FIXED PERIOD OF GESTATION

A baby will always take about nine months to grow and a carrot will always germinate at around ninety days. There is a very small margin of deviation and usually, those are the figures. A carrot seed has a fixed vibration; it can only vibrate to the frequency of a carrot seed. But people can become whoever they want to become and so, when it comes to manifesting from thought-forms, the gestation period is not as fixed. It fluctuates because our thoughts, desires, and feelings are constantly changing. In other words, the gestation period will vary from person to person because people are individuals with free will and so the time it takes to reap the reward will differ.

"Have patience. Allah does not deny the rewards of the righteous."

– The Holy Qur'an [11:115]

THE FOUR ESSENTIALS

The speed of the process depends on four things: The intensity of one's desire, the steadiness of the one's faith, the efficiency of one's actions, and the depth of one's gratitude.

o Desire: A desire is a strong feeling of wanting something to happen.

o Faith: Having complete trust in something.

o Gratitude: The quality of being thankful, and of showing appreciation.

o Efficient action: Making sure each action is done in an efficient manner.

"There is nothing more essential in life than the mastery of the four essentials."

WHAT WE WILL WORK ON

Working knowledge and a good understanding of the principles that constitute how the law of attraction works will also speed up the process considerably. Throughout the book, we will work on intensifying your desire, cultivating your faith, inducing an attitude of gratitude, and increasing the efficiency of your actions. You will possess these four things necessary for conscious manifestation and you will also be equipped with, and have at your disposal, working knowledge of how the law of attraction works and how to use it effectively in your life. You will be provided with affirmations and quotes to reprogram your subconscious beliefs, which will ultimately forge the walls of positivity around your mind to shut out all negative suggestions and external negative influences.

"We don't see things as they are. We see things as we are."

- Anais Nin

IT BEGINS WITH THOUGHT

The law of attraction will bring to you the people, objects, and situations which are a vibrational match to the frequency of your predominant thoughts and feelings. It is not so much your thoughts which attract to you the things you desire, but more so your feelings. However, thought is the starting point because thoughts are what induce feelings and so thoughts are what sets the energy in motion to attract and to bring to you the things that you want. All creation originates from thought-forms. All manifestation and circumstances of life begin as an intangible impulse of energy. All creation begins with a desire; a desire to do, to have, or to become. By changing your thoughts, you will change your belief system, which will, in turn, change how you perceive and how you feel. When this occurs, your actions will be based on that new belief system and that new level of awareness. Your actions will be what dictate the habits you form, and your habits will attract the like effect that is a vibrational match to the root cause of the habit.

"Man becomes what he thinks about all day long."

– Ralph Waldo Emerson

THE FIVE-STEP PROCESS

Our circumstances of life are the result of a five-step process. The process consists of thoughts, feelings, actions, habits, and circumstance. I will give you an example of how it works.

"Positive thoughts induce positive feelings. Positive feelings cause positive actions. Positive actions create positive habits, and positive habits crystallize into the circumstance of positivity."

"Negative thoughts induce negative feelings. Negative feelings cause negative actions. Negative actions create negative habits, and negative habits crystallize into the circumstance of negativity."

We are creatures of habit. And, since our circumstances are the results of our habits, which were created by our actions in response to our feelings, which, in turn, were the result of our thoughts, it is safe to say then that a man's complete circumstance of life is the result of that which he has thought. And all that man is, does, or has, is the direct result of that which he thinks about. And so, our reality is literally the outward physical expression of our inward non-physical impression of thought.

> "Man is but a product of his thoughts, what he thinks he becomes."
>
> -Mahatma Gandhi

THE ANALOGY OF THE WRITER

Let's suppose you wish to attract to you the reality in which you are the writer of a best-selling book. The first goal would be to plant that desire into your mind by thinking like a writer. These thoughts will become repetitive until you begin to feel like an author. Then, because you feel like one, you will naturally begin to act like one. Your actions will be in alignment with what a writer does day in day out. These actions will become repetitive until they form habitual behaviour. The habit of writing will crystallize into the circumstance of being a writer.

At this point, you are only a writer, however, you still need to attract to you the circumstance of being the author of a best-selling book. This is where the four essentials come to your aid. Intense desire, unwavering faith, devout gratitude, and efficient action.

A lot of writers are a failure, there is no doubt about that. But they are a failure because they are lacking in either of the four essentials. They have formed the habit of being a writer but they lack either one or more of the higher vision, the faith in attaining the vision, the attitude of gratitude, or the efficiency of action necessary. They only see themselves writing, but they do not see themselves writing a best-selling book. Their circumstance is built off the belief that their writing will not be a success; they are operating on a failure frequency because they expect failure. And, quite simply because they lack faith. This lack of vision and faith will ultimately prevent them from taking efficient action and it will certainly cause insufficiency in their gratitude. The law of attraction will only attract more of what's held in the image of their mind and according to what they currently believe. They may even be grateful for what they currently receive, but gratitude will only be of benefit and attract better to you if aligned with faith and a higher vision. A lack of faith and higher vision prevents these writers from becoming efficient which will ultimately prevent them from becoming great writers. And the disappointment in not becoming a great writer will usually have the effect of dissolving one's attitude of gratitude. It's a vicious cycle and so, as you can see, it is not enough to form the habit—that is only one part. The four essentials are essential.

You need a clear mental picture of the things you wish to do, to own, or to become. Then you must couple this picture with an unwavering faith that the image you hold in your mind will be attained. You must· have faith in yourself and in the universe. With faith comes a higher level of awareness, which will, in turn, allow for the efficient action necessary to take the right steps towards your mental image. This will instil in your mind even more confidence and it will increase your already-unwavering faith, thus allowing you to easily express the attitude of gratitude based on the belief and expectation that the reality is being given to you.

"Burning desire backed by faith knows no such word as impossible."

– Napoleon Hill

DIGGING DEEPER INTO THE LAW OF ATTRACTION

So, let's go deeper into what the law of attraction is and how it actually works. All people, objects, and circumstances of life are currently operating on their own particular frequency. Through the law of attraction, you pull to you only the people, objects, and circumstances that are vibrating at the same frequency. The frequency of our thoughts dictates who we attract, what we attract, and what circumstances of life we will experience. You can only experience the things that are a vibrational match to the frequency of your predominant thoughts. Everything outside of that vibrational frequency exists on a different channel, and to pull them to you, you must change the vibration of your thoughts to obtain the frequency that matches the experiences or circumstances of life which you want to experience.

If you imagine that you wish to call a friend who lives on the other side of the globe. Irrespective of the distance, you can get into contact with this person; it doesn't matter if your friend is in Canada, USA, India, China, or Australia, your phone can tune into their phone and you can both communicate as though you were in the same room. If you are at home in the UK and you wish to phone a friend in the USA, you must align your devices up to the same frequency. As soon as you enter your friend's unique number into your phone, you align up the frequency of your device to the frequency of theirs. And just like that, your call connects and in an instant, you are now in conversation with your friend.

The law of attraction operates the same way. It doesn't matter what you want, and it doesn't matter how far away that reality seems, irrespective of distance, you can pull those things to you. Because the frequencies operate outside of time and space. There is no distance, and there is nothing too large or too small that the law of attraction cannot bring to you. It is only our thinking that makes it so. The only reason why they seem so far away for you right now is that your thoughts are operating on a different frequency. And from that frequency—from that level of awareness—you are not aware of anything beyond the frequency which you are currently operating at. But there is no distance between frequencies, it is just a slight shift in consciousness. It is as easy to manifest a house as it is a phone. It just depends on whether you are focused on a house or a phone. The infinite power of the universe doesn't know the difference between the house or the phone. It is only according to your faith will it be brought to you. Our belief that one will take longer than the other to attract is due to our own self-imposed limitations and is the result of our belief system which we have acquired since birth. Since birth, you have been taught limitation, lack, and have been handed down the belief that if you are to attain the things you want, it will be at the expense of struggle and hard work. This inherent belief system exists in you because it exists in the collective consciousness.

> "Our only limitations are the ones we set up in our own minds."
>
> – Napoleon Hill

THE COLLECTIVE CONSCIOUSNESS

The 100th monkey effect is a phenomenon which was observed by psychologists during an experiment. The experiment was conducted in the 1950s and it spanned for over 30 years. In this experiment, the researchers would give a tribe of Japanese snow monkeys sweet potatoes to eat, however, they were covered in sand. The monkeys loved the potatoes, but the dry sand wasn't too pleasant on their pallets. After a while, one of the monkeys learned that if she washed the potatoes in a nearby stream then the sand would be removed from the potato. Although many were still eating the sand-covered potatoes, it wasn't long before many of the monkeys began to copy the washing technique, and so the majority began to learn the method of washing the potatoes. Then something unexpected happened. Let's just say there were 99 monkeys on this island that were using the technique. When one more monkey learned the technique, and when one more monkey began to wash the potatoes, a critical mass was reached and suddenly all the monkeys on the island knew the technique and all the monkeys were washing the potatoes before eating them. Not only that, but tribes of monkeys across the sea, located on distant islands, automatically picked up the technique and they, too, were washing the potatoes before eating them. This experiment shows that when a certain number of monkeys became aware, and when a certain critical mass was achieved, this awareness was communicated from mind to mind. And so, when only a limited number are aware of a new technique or possibility, it remains a conscious property of only those few. However, when a critical mass is achieved and when the level of awareness is increased by just one more individual who tunes into it, then the conscious field is strengthened enough so that the awareness can be picked up by almost everyone.

All specimens are connected to their own species. It's why birds naturally fly in formation. It's why ants all know how to work together. It's why all specimens generally act in the same way and conduct themselves in a similar manner to the rest of their species. It's why an orangutan knows which plant is poisonous, and it's also why all animals know how to defend themselves without ever attending an animal martial arts class. Evolution has equipped all species with the ability to carry over the knowledge of their ancestors. Knowledge acquired and accumulated throughout the history of the species is held within the collective consciousness to avoid the specimens of the species making unnecessary mistakes that might threaten their survival. And the same is true with humans. Within the human collective consciousness, there is an accumulation of our ancestors' beliefs consisting of what is believed to be possible and reflecting on where our current awareness is at as a collective. In this collective conscious is held all the beliefs of the people of the world today based on what was believed by the people who came before us. The limitations and what we believe to be possible is held here.

Before the plane was invented, the belief held in the human collective conscious was that an aircraft was impossible. When the Wright brothers got a plane into the air, and when enough people saw that it was possible and accepted it as true, then the critical level of awareness was reached enough to update the collective consciousness which was to accept the aircraft as a possibility and, ultimately, pass the awareness to the majority of the members of the species.

Before the mile was run in under 4 minutes, the collective conscious was tuned into the frequency of awareness which labelled the feat impossible. And nobody could do it. Until in 1954 when Roger Bannister ran the mile in 3 minutes 59 seconds. Once this feat was observed, and once our species knew it to be possible, and once the critical mass was reached, it wasn't long before others were running the mile in under 4 minutes. It wasn't even 2 months later in fact.

And since then, the record set by Roger Bannister has been beaten by a further 17 seconds. This all happened because Roger Bannister was able to pull himself beyond the boundaries of human belief and expectancy. And, in doing so, he paved the way for others to pull away too.

Held within this collective consciousness is all the limitations and beliefs of the human race. Since 80% operate on a negative frequency, the collective conscious is tipped towards the side of negativity and a lower level of awareness. You can transcend your awareness beyond the negativity, the limitations, and the collective beliefs. But that is why you must consciously learn to turn the dial and tune into what you desire purposely. For if you leave it on autopilot, it will tune into the awareness and the frequency of the collective—which you do not want to happen. The collective consciousness is vibrating to the frequency of fear, doubt, and worry. However, we can instead tune ourselves into the frequency of faith, certainty, and peace. 20% of the world tune into that today, and in the future when the 20% reaches 51%, the balance will tip and you can then run on autopilot. But until then, it will be of no benefit to you.

> "When you are writing your story of life, don't let anyone else hold the pen."

THE DOUBLE-SLIT EXPERIMENT

The double-slit experiment is a phenomenon in which quantum physicists have observed that a conscious observer has an effect on the behaviour of an electron. Imagine a steel sheet that has two slits carved out of it about three inches apart and behind this sheet, picture a wall. Now, if you imagine an electron gun firing electrons through the slits, the logical thing would be to expect that on the wall behind the sheet, there would be a corresponding pattern that represents which slit the electron went through. But this wasn't the case. Instead, they found an interference pattern. The pattern didn't seem to correspond to the slit in which the electron went through and so they believed the electrons were interfering with one another. However, they then began to fire the electrons one at a time and much to their dismay, the same interference occurred. It was as if the electron breaks itself up and goes through both the slits and no slit all at the same time. This baffled physicists and so they began to use a detector to attempt to see what was going on. But the strangest part about it is that when using the detector, the electron went through only the slit which it had been fired through. There was now no interference pattern. Almost as if the electron knew it was being watched, it acted in the way in which it was expected to act. Without any observation, the electron acted out all potentialities simultaneously. However, when a conscious observer was observing it, the electron only presented the potentiality which aligned with that which the conscious observer expected to happen. The universe will always present to you exactly what you subconsciously expect to be presented with.

"Energy flows where attention goes."

– Tony Robbins

HOW TO USE THE LAW OF ATTRACTION

To explain how to use the law of attraction, we will now refer back to the analogy of the garden. Your mind is the soil, your desire is the seed, the water is your actions, and the sun is your feelings. First, you must clear the mind of any negatives, you must cultivate the soil of your mind and dig out any weeds to ensure it is receptive for the seed of desire to be planted. Then, you must nurture the seed with regular watering by continuous, efficient action towards the germination of the seed. In the meantime, you need to keep the sun shining; the sun is your unwavering faith that the seed will germinate and your willingness to entertain lively gratitude for the blessings of the germinated seed.

"Therefore, I say to you. Whatever things you ask for when you pray, believe that you receive them, and you shall have them."

– Mark [11:24]

THE WORKINGS OF THE MIND

To understand how to use the law of attraction consciously, it would be of benefit to possess a working knowledge of the human mind and brain and to further understand the process of thought transmission. Anyone familiar with the works of Napoleon Hill will know that the brain is both a broadcasting and receiving station for thought transmission. To understand this process of transmission, we need to become familiar with the principles of the conscious mind, the subconscious mind, autosuggestion, creative imagination, and infinite intelligence.

> "My brain is only a receiver, in the universe there is a core from which we obtain knowledge, strength and inspiration. I have not penetrated the secrets to this core, but I know that it exists."
>
> -Nikola Tesla

THOUGHT REVISITED

As we discovered in the previous section on thought, thoughts are impulses of energy. There is one truth in which all philosophers, scientists, and theologians agree on—that energy cannot be created or destroyed. Energy can only transmute from one form into another. Because of this, we now know that thoughts, being energy, cannot be created or destroyed. And so, thoughts are not something which our brains create. Thoughts have a frequency and we tune into the particular frequency of thought. In other words, we do not create our thoughts, none of us do. We pick them out and tune into the thoughts that already exist.

"Energy cannot be created or destroyed."

INFINITE INTELLIGENCE

Infinite intelligence, infinite awareness, the ether, the core, the formless, consciousness, source, God. It has been given many names, but they all refer to the same power. The power that follows night with day and summer with winter. The power which causes water to flow downstream in response to gravity, that which converts acorns into oak trees. This power keeps our hearts beating for us without our conscious effort. It heals our cuts, digests our food, and it turns a single cell that is not visible to the human eye into a fully-grown human being. In this universe, there is an intelligence and there is no doubt about it. This intelligence is eternal, universal, and infinite. It is a thinking substance; a substance that thinks. It consists of energy. The purest form of energy there is. It is from this substance which everything else derives. The comprehension of this intelligence paralyzes one's reason. It is the uncaused cause of all that is. All potentialities, all arrangement of matter, all thought vibrations which can exist, do exist, and will exist, resides there. The power is simply awareness, and it connects to your conscious mind.

> "It is a simple procedure to say how many seeds there are in an apple. But who among us could ever say how many apples there are in a seed?"

THE CONSCIOUS MIND

The conscious mind is the reasoning portion of the mind and it is the receiving station in the process of thought transmission. It's the part of your mind that thinks, and which makes decisions. The conscious mind is aware of its surroundings; it receives thoughts from sense impressions that have been picked up through our daily environment AND infinite intelligence through the faculty of the creative imagination, which arrive in the form of pictures and ideas. The conscious mind acts as an outer guard to the approach of the subconscious mind to protect it from false impressions.

> "The mind moves in the direction of our predominant thoughts."
>
> -Earl Nightingale

THE SUBCONSCIOUS MIND

The subconscious mind is the intuitive portion of the mind and it is the sending station in the process of thought transmission. It doesn't think, it doesn't choose—it just acts on the thoughts which are passed on to it from the conscious mind. The subconscious is impressionable; it cannot reject a thought which is passed to it either by belief, emotionalization, or repetition. It accepts any thought that makes it through as fact and acts upon it. The subconscious mind acts on thoughts that have been repeated or emotionalized through autosuggestion.

> "Any thought repeated often enough and convincingly enough is finally accepted by the subconscious mind."
>
> - Napoleon Hill

AUTOSUGGESTION

Autosuggestion is habitual self-suggestion; it is the inner dialogue that operates within the conscious mind. It is the voice that communicates with your subconscious mind and is the tool which is used to command the subconscious mind. Through the use of autosuggestion, your conscious mind programs your subconscious mind and it does this through emotionalization and repetition of thought.

> "It's not what you say out your mouth that determines your life, it's what you whisper to yourself that has the most power."
>
> -Robert Kiyosaki

THE CREATIVE IMAGINATION

The creative imagination is one of the six mental faculties of the mind. It operates in the conscious mind and is the faculty in which the conscious mind receives thoughts and ideas in the form of pictures. The creative imagination is limitless; it is only limited to the extent to which the faculty has been developed in the mind of the person in which it operates. Anything that is received by way of the creative imagination can be transmuted into its physical counterpart. The transmutation is in accordance with, and subject to, the individual's belief.

"Whatever the mind can conceive and believe, the mind can achieve."

-Napoleon Hill

THE SIX BASIC FEARS

I now wish to speak about fear because fear is a virus in of itself—it spreads like wildfire. It is the worst affliction to suffer from, for it weakens the immune system, invites disease, attracts negativity, and it causes temporary insanity. Fear does serve a purpose, but only in a very few rare instances and when under an immediate threat. The six basic fears prevalent in humans from most common to least are the fear of poverty, the fear of criticism, the fear of ill health, the fear of loss of love, the fear of old age, and the fear of death. The fear of poverty is the most common fear because if poverty was to strike, it increases the likelihood of the other five fears occurring. If one is poor, it invites criticism from others who are doing better, it welcomes ill health due to a lack of cleanliness and nutrition, it provides reason for a loved one to leave, it paralyzes one at the prospect of growing old in that condition, and it will increase the likelihood of death due to all the above. In this book, we will remedy these irrational fears. It would be of benefit to add here that if you are able to stamp out the fear of poverty and the fear of death, then quite naturally, the other 4 fears begin to fade into nothingness.

"Fear is the biggest virus of them all."

UNDERSTANDING A VIRUS

There are two major forms of a virus. An RNA virus and a DNA virus. An RNA virus is any virus in which the genetic information is stored in the form of RNA, as opposed to DNA. An RNA virus contains ribonucleic acid as its genetic material. A DNA virus contains nucleic acid as its genetic material. The main difference between an RNA virus and a DNA virus is the sugar which is present in the molecules. The sugar present in an RNA molecule is ribose, whereas the sugar present in the molecule of a DNA virus is deoxyribose. RNA viruses generally have higher mutation rates in comparison to DNA viruses because viral RNA polymerases lack the proofreading ability of DNA polymerases. Proofreading ability refers to the virus' ability to correct itself. Examples of RNA viruses include Ebola virus, rabies, SARS, the common cold, influenza, hepatitis C, hepatitis E, West Nile fever, polio, measles, and coronavirus.

A QUICK MESSAGE TO YOU

The next few parts I wasn't going to add into this book for two reasons. Firstly, because quite simply I don't wish to scare anybody and I do not wish to detract from the positivity of the book. The aim of the book is to eradicate fear, doubt, and worry, and to teach you how to use the universal laws in order to remain safe. With this being the case, I believed the next parts may work as counterproductive to the very essence of this work. Secondly, a lot of people are just not ready to hear it and simply will refuse to accept it. But on the other hand, there are many people who are ready to hear it and who are ready to accept it, and it's because of them that I have decided to write about it. It took me a while to come to that decision. I sat for hours pondering whether or not I should, but my last words directly before making the decision were, and I quote, "Fuck it, let's get it done". I made the decision because I believe it's only right to add this part in, for I concluded that it may also prove helpful in many ways more than one. Besides, it is of no secret anymore and a fair amount of the world has awoken to this truth.

I would like to reassure you here that the power of the universal laws are unrivalled and if you possess the knowledge of the universal laws, and if you apply them, then what you are about to hear will make no difference whatsoever. The dark truths that follow are minuscule in comparison to the power that lies within you and to the things that you can accomplish in using that power. And when you begin to realise that what you are about to hear has only been accomplished through the knowledge of the universal laws, then it shall reassure you to know that after reading this book, you too shall have that knowledge in your possession. So, let's get this dark part over with so we can swiftly get back to doing that which we do best, and that is focusing on the light.

"If God be for us, then who can be against us?" -

Romans [8:31]

THE PLOT THICKENS

There is a plot. And a very sinister plot indeed. This plot goes by the name of the New World Order. Right here on earth, there is a hidden hand that controls the money, religion, the stock market, the politics, the media, and the education system. This hidden hand has in their possession a working knowledge of the universal laws and they have an understanding that the majority of the world simply do not. But that knowledge has been and will be presented in this book. Back of this hand is an elite few, the 0.1% who, by controlling these sources, control what we think, believe, and do. Through these sources, they control the collective consciousness and thus dictate the reality in which we experience as a collective.

Throughout human existence, there has been a prevalent desire in man to conquer and control the earth. In pursuit of this desire, empires have been built and lost. All the wars of the past, the present, and the future are nothing more than man's quest for ultimate power and control. Behind this desire lies the emotion of greed and the selfish want for man to obtain power over his fellow men. Due to the many failed attempts, it was soon discovered that leadership by force will not endure for very long, for the people will eventually rebel and the power and control that they desire will once again be out of reach. However, these people soon realised that if the people were made to believe that they were free—if the people were not controlled through force or through physical means—then the people would not resist, for they would have no idea they were being controlled in the first place.

Leadership by consent will endure, and to control the minds of the masses through psychological slavery is a much easier feat and it subtlety allows for them to slowly but surely, little by little, claim the liberty of the people in exchange for protection and a modicum of temporary security.

Using the sources of control mentioned above, they systematically play on humanity's six basic fears to slowly implement their sinister hidden agenda. They have one goal and one goal only. That is to create a centralised power, a global centralised infrastructure. Quite simply, they wish to create a one-world government. This one-world government is to operate using a global currency with a singular one-world military. The currency is to be digital, and it will be implemented using an RFID chip, i.e. a radio frequency identification chip, which is to be implanted under the skin of the human being. It is to become a means of mass tracking and it is to give them complete control of the money. By having this control, it allows them to deduct money at will and monitor all transactions. A cashless society will further divide people in the sense that no money can be borrowed from individual to individual. The amount you have is the amount you will get, and there is no way around it. If you fail to comply or if you wish to protest, then the chip gets deactivated which ultimately ejects you from the ranks of society, leaving you with no food, no water, and no means of getting any. Complete control of the people.

The military is to be singular, and it will be trained to protect the establishment and to protect the infrastructure. They aim to strip away individuality by removing free will and by merging countries and culture into one. They wish to build just one global power that imposes one set of laws while controlling all access to earth's resources and information. This system will be one of ultimate surveillance and A.I. will do most of the work. Through the RFID chip and facial recognition systems that will be set up in every street, every movement, action, transaction, and interaction will be monitored, and it will be recorded.

These plans have been in fruition now for many, many years. Hundreds in fact. And it really began to pick up pace in 1913 upon the creation of the federal reserve banking system. Prior to this, money had value. You could be exchanged gold at banks in return for your money. You could essentially walk into a bank with your twenty-pound note and receive its equivalent in gold. The bank promised to pay the bearer the sum of the amount in gold. Now, with inflation, our money is essentially worthless and the likelihood of receiving any reasonable amount of gold is basically zero. The only reason it holds value is because of our belief that it has value. When the belief goes, well, the banks will close up shop.

The hidden hand which controls the governments employ a special tactic and it goes like this: create a problem, cause a reaction, provide a solution. In 1929, in the US, they created a problem in the form of a great depression. This problem created a reaction; the reaction was intense fear running through the minds of every man, woman, and child due to the fear of poverty. And remember, this fear opens up the door to the other five basic fears. Once they got the reaction, they provided them with a solution. The solution was, to get out of the depression, every man and woman must hand in their gold. All Americans were required by law to turn in their gold on or before May 1, 1933, to the federal reserve in return for $20.67 of paper money per troy ounce. Americans who did not turn in their gold were subject to arrest on criminal charges and faced up to 10 years in federal prison.

So, you see from this instance how they work. They wanted gold, so they created a problem, caused a reaction, and then provided a solution that resonates with their aim. A solution to a problem which they, themselves, covertly created. It was daylight robbery. And, as you can imagine, after the robbery was carried out, the depression ended, and everything resumed back to normal. People will do whatever it takes to avoid the six basic fears, and if that means parting with gold then so be it. But there is another thing that people will part with to avoid the six basic fears, and that is freedom.

Freedoms are freely given away in exchange for security. People fear the 6 fears so much so that, in order to avoid facing them, they will hand over essential liberties. Propaganda will cause the collective consciousness to vibrate at such a fearful frequency and to such an extent that it will systematically play into the hands of those who seek even more power. They will continuously play on the six basic human fears which will, in turn, separate our society who will, unfortunately, begin to fear one another. In times of crisis, power is up for grabs. Liberties can be taken in exchange for security, and in exchange for temporary protection from that crisis. A global crisis can also have other benefits too; it can serve as a tool of distraction and it can be used as a means of misdirection. While the world's attention is on a crisis, the powers that be are free to explore other avenues and further an agenda which may have been impossible without the misdirection.

While under mass house arrest, or in its polite form, 'lockdown' as it has been commonly referred to, the powers that be have leveraged the distraction caused by 'coronavirus' and they have used it as a means of instilling and introducing many new acts; acts which further extend their power. During this time, a bill was passed which allows for the exercise of new emergency powers such as mandatory quarantines, forced vaccinations, and injectable biosensors. Not to mention the fact that the whole situation is classically conditioning us to the normality of self-isolation.

The crisis also serves as a necessary component to the intentional aim of driving the currency into the ground, which they will do, which, in fact, they have already done. As mentioned in a preceding paragraph, our money is essentially worthless and when the belief in the money goes, the markets will collapse, and recession will hit. Out of fear, the world will beg for a solution. And of course, they will have one, one which fits their hidden agenda. A solution designed to strip away yet more freedom, privacy, and one which further extends their quest for power and ultimate control. This solution will arrive by way of a digital currency in the form of a radio frequency identification chip, as mentioned earlier. Facial recognition will line our streets, police drones will fly our skies, and 5G towers will be set up at every turn.

5G towers popped up everywhere during the coronavirus lockdown. One of the many bills that is being passed is one that provides them with the power to set up 5G masts. 5G is untested and extremely dangerous, you may have seen or heard about the birds throughout the country dropping stark dead, falling from the sky due to the unbearable frequencies which it emits. 4G radiation emits on average 3-5 GHz, whereas 5G operates on frequencies of up to a ridiculous 60GHz and I don't know if I need to further explain, but that is simply not safe. Why would they do that? Because the plot thickens. 5G will need to eventually be abolished. We must create a reality without 5G, it has had its very short time. It will be detrimental to our health and so, we should focus on creating something better. I can't emphasize that point enough.

The world will be released from 'Saving Lives Penitentiary', and they will step out into the light once again, they will stretch their arms, maybe give a little yawn, and then they will smile in belief that the world is their oyster. They will commence their day with the notion that the world is the same as it was before they went in. But this is not the case. We are walking out into the beginning of a long-planned dystopian future. Into the beginnings of a sinister new normal; and the extremely dangerous frequencies that will be penetrating through our brains whilst radiating through our skin will be coherently screaming: "Welcome to the New World Order".

To create a global power, one must first create a global problem. That problem must cause a global reaction so that it opens the doors to the induction of a global solution. Coronavirus should be the least of your concerns, for that is just the problem which was intentionally created. The laws which will be passed because of coronavirus—now that's what you need to watch out for.

They say a few people can't take over the world, they say it's much too difficult. I say, if they have people fighting over toilet rolls… who said that they can't?

The implementation of a global centralised power definitely isn't easy, however. It takes time, persistence, calculation, and it takes a divide and conquer tactic that is very subtle but most definitely, very effective. After all, it's a game of chess, not checkers.

"People willing to trade their freedom for temporary security deserve neither and will lose both."

– Benjamin Franklin

POPULATION CONTROL

The plot mentioned above isn't the part which I believe is the sinister part of all this. The unsettling part about the whole thing is that within this new world order, it seems like they do not want us all to be in it. No, they want to select the right candidates. And the right candidates are those who they can easily control. Anybody outside of that criteria simply does not make the grade. Furthermore, they cannot have complete control over seven billion people, and they know that very well. However, they can control half a billion, or at least, they seem to think that they can. For this is the number that the "Georgia Guidestones" indicates. The Georgia Guidestones is a monument that stands at an approximate elevation of 750 feet above sea level, about 140 km east of Atlanta, 72 km from Athens Georgia, and 14 km north of the centre of the city of Elberton. The monument is almost twice the size of Stonehenge and its construction used almost a quarter of a million pounds of granite. No one knows who paid for the construction of the Georgia Guidestones, nor what is meant by the strange messages engraved on them. The "Message of the Georgia Guidestones" seems to call for at least 90% of the Earth's population to be wiped out. The passage about maintaining humanity at a population of a half-billion or less would require a massive dying-off of humanity. This is what has led many to allege that whoever financed the Guidestones, are in with an evil New World Order project to extensively depopulate the planet. The stones were defaced with graffiti in 2008. The spray-painted message was "death to the new world order". Depopulation will take many forms, and biological warfare in the form of vaccination will be one of them.

"If we do a really great job on vaccines and reproductive health services, we could lower the world population by perhaps 10% or 15%."

- Bill Gates

BIOLOGICAL WARFARE

Biological warfare is the use of weaponised bacteria that are administered via vaccination. The United States biological weapons program officially began in spring of 1943 on orders from U.S. President Franklin Roosevelt. Research continued following World War II. During this time, the U.S. built up a large stockpile of biological agents and weapons and throughout its 27-year history, the program weaponised and stockpiled the following seven bio-agents: anthrax, tularaemia, brucellosis, Q-fever, VEE, botulism, and staphylococcal. They also engaged in the research of many more.

Since then, the methods have become much more sophisticated. The age of technology in combination with the many years of research has accelerated the scientific breakthroughs and has increased the lethality of this method of war. In the form of 'vaccines', they now possess advanced forms of bio-warfare that can target specific Geno types. This basically transforms bio-warfare from the realm of terror into a useful political tool. These newer advanced forms are researched within an organisation that was created to supposedly protect society in light of an epidemic.

"I am going to vaccinate the world for its own good."

-Bill Gates

CENTRE FOR DISEASE CONTROL

The Centre for Disease Control is an organisation that was set up with the role of preventing disease and managing outbreaks. It is here where research is done on diseases, and it is where new diseases are formulated. The Pirbright Institute, which is partially funded by the Bill and Melinda Gates Foundation, owns a patent on a strain of coronavirus and other viruses including African swine fever virus. The patent is listed as a vaccine. Furthermore, the U.S. Centre for Disease Control owns a patent on another strain of coronavirus, patent number US7220852B1, which is listed for the severe acute respiratory syndrome, also known as SARS.

According to Bill and Melinda Gates, they bought the rights for humanitarian purposes, but not everyone agrees with that claim. The patent page on coronavirus explains that it may be used as a means of vaccinating diseases such as bronchitis. Bill Gates delivered a TED Talk where he outlined his plan to "vaccinate the world, for its own good". India recently Gave the Gates Foundation the boot after learning that children in remote villages were being used as human guinea pigs and were in effect dying as a result of the unproven vaccines. The members of the emergency epidemic board who attended Event 201 included representatives from the UN, China, The Gates Foundation, Centre for Disease Control, Johnson and Johnson, logistical powerhouses, and the media. Six weeks later, the apposed strain of coronavirus from Wuhan, China was unveiled to the general public and the Gates Foundation pledged $10 million to help fight the coronavirus; one similar to that which they hold a patent on.

The coronavirus was created by man in the Centre for Disease Control. It is a weaponised strain of virus that is not contagious through the air but is instead to be administered as a deadly vaccine

"A coming disease could kill thirty million people in six months."

– Bill Gates

ELECTRONIC WARFARE

The WHO/UN Agenda 21/30 Depopulation Plan via 5G 60 GHz millimetre waves and toxic coronavirus vaccine injections.

Airborne contagious viruses do not exist and are not planned or escaped bioweapons from secret government labs. Germs, bacteria, and virus proteins are created inside your body and they are created by your body. They are not contagious. The only way to get foreign human or animal bacterial and viral tissue inside your body is by injection. You simply cannot catch or ingest animal virus proteins from eating sick bats and pigs. The stomach and intestinal enzymes turn them into amino acids and di/tripeptides. Just ask the thousands upon thousands of scientists and medical professionals who are saying the same thing. 60 GHz millimetre radiation waves from 5G towers create the same bodily distress symptoms as the fake coronavirus. These radiation waves also create the same exact protein/nucleic acid response in your body from the resulting tissue damage. The same damage that these coronavirus 'tests' are supposedly looking for. The patented coronavirus 'vaccine' will indeed have toxic foreign human or animal hybrid viral proteins in it as well as dozens of other dangerous toxins.

As 5G 60 GHz millimetre wave towers get switched on in more and more cities, they need a scapegoat for the mass deaths and respiratory illnesses that will follow. They need you to believe at all costs that it is the coronavirus and not the 5G towers which are killing people. They care not if you believe it came from eating bat soup or if you caught it from a neighbour. They don't even care if you believe it's a secret government bio-weapon that was purposely released from the centre of disease control. Just as long as you are ignorant to the truth that coronavirus doesn't exist at all; except in the lab-created vaccine that they will inject you with later. They need you to believe it's real, they need you to believe it's airborne, and they need you to believe it's contagious. That way, you will go willingly into a quarantine camp if you are to be targeted as undesirable by those behind Agenda 21/30.

The coronavirus is a scapegoat, a con and a cover-up to the deaths that are being caused by 5G radiation. They have been set up to further an agenda of control and to kill off thousands, if not millions of people in the process. Problem. Reaction. Solution. The invisible enemy that is coronavirus is the problem; the reaction is fear and the solution will be a mandatory vaccination and a cashless society.

The continued deaths from 5G radiation will be cause enough to turn the public against anybody who rejects the deadly vaccine. They will be labelled a threat to society and it will not be tolerated. It is a very subtle yet very effective divide and conquer tactic. The vaccine will be used to mutate the human DNA, it will cause problems with conception and reproductivity to aid in population control and it will further work in conjunction with the RFID chip to create a digital identification. Big Pharma and Microsoft have teamed up on this project and it is called 'ID2020 Alliance'.

With technological capabilities constantly improving, it hasn't taken them long to capitalise on the advancement of it by weaponizing that technology in pursuit of their insidious agenda.

"We are on the verge of a global transformation. It only takes the right major crisis and the nations will accept the new world order."

– David Rockefeller

THE MEDIA

The media is a tool that is used as a means of spreading propaganda which aligns with the aims of the hidden agenda. It is a tool which is used to spread misinformation. Its purpose is to misinform, misdirect, and keep the collective consciousness in a frequency of negativity and fear. In 1983, 90% of the media was owned by 50 companies. As of 2011, 90% of the media is controlled by only six companies. The media is the most powerful tool in their possession because, through this tool, they can enhance the power of their other tools. This tool labels people, divides them, misdirects them, causes petty controversies, instils fear, pushes agenda, and programs the public on what to think. There is a reason why they call it a television 'programme'. The ultimate goal, as stated, is to keep the collective consciousness vibrating at a frequency of awareness which suits their means and aids their hidden agenda.

"The media's the most powerful entity on earth. They have the ability to make the innocent guilty and make the guilty innocent, and that's power. Because they control the minds of the masses."

– Malcolm X

BACK TO THE LIGHT

Right, now that's over with, we can come back to the light. But before we do, I would just like to say that if the ideas in the preceding paragraphs were new to you, it may have been quite a scary read and I want you to know that I completely understand how you feel. I, too, went through the same experience many years ago. The very essence of the experience sparks the emotion of unbelief. That is a completely normal reaction. This book is designed to empower you and so it is your choice and your choice alone as to whether you buy into the ideas or not. If having the knowledge of what's going on in the world empowers you, then retain the knowledge. If poring over it is too painful for you or if you wish not to believe it, then disregard it at your own will. The great thing is that no matter what you decide to believe, it will in no way hinder your progress in making use of the universal laws which are outlined in this book. Always come to your own decisions, never let anybody tell you what to think. Always do what is best for you at the time because the truth is, nobody knows what's right for you, but you. I have put the knowledge forward to quite simply give you a chance. And in doing so, they will probably seek to tarnish my reputation and I must add here that I wholeheartedly welcome them to try.

I will now restate a truth which was outlined in 'A quick message to you' just to bring your mind back to where we were before we entered into the 'darkness'. It is important that you remember this message, so here it is again:

I would like to reassure you here that the power of the universal laws are unrivalled and if you possess the knowledge of the universal laws, and if you apply them, then what you just heard will make no difference. The 'dark' truths are minuscule in comparison to the creative power that lies within you and to the things that you can accomplish in using that power. When you begin to realise that what you just heard is only being accomplished through the knowledge of the universal laws, then it shall reassure you to know that after reading this book, you, too, shall have that knowledge in your possession.

Throughout the next two parts of this book, you will be equipped with the understandings that will free you from fear, doubt, and worry.

> "Darkness and Evil have no actuality of their own. They are just an appearance. The appearance of darkness is simply the absence of light. The appearance of evil is simply an absence of love. Only light exists, and only love. They exist on an infinite scale and to infinite degrees. Darkness and evil are just a lack of; they appear as a result of being at the lower end of the spectrum and at a lower degree."

IT'S ALL PART OF THE DIVINE PLAN

It is all a part of the divine plan. The universe operates according to law and order; it never operates according to disorder and chance. All the seemingly negative aspects of life are but part of a much deeper positive aspect and a greater plan. They are a necessary component in the unfoldment and advancement of the human species. The God force that is in all things cannot impede its own evolution; it must let us come up and it must let us transcend our inadequacies by ourselves. We have been blessed with free will and to impose on, and intervene in, our affairs would be contradictory to the very essence of the purpose of life. No matter what conditions arise here on earth, no matter what appears, be it 'good' or 'bad', just know that it is perfect in itself. They are perfect for their time, for what they are, and they are essential to our growth.

The universe is justly ordered, nothing is out of place and nothing should be changed. To fight creation is to compete with it; fighting against an appearance is to simply disagree with the truth of what is. It only causes you to kick, whine, and push against our collective creation, which is counterproductive and of little use. To change conditions here on earth, our job is not to focus on fighting the old but instead, focus on building the new. For, to accept where we are and to thrive from that place with the goal to create better, is to be in alignment with our evolution and in alignment to the true nature of our being.

The world today is exactly how it needs to be—it could be no other way. What is, simply is. The belief that things should somehow be different or that some things are out of place is an erroneous belief. We live in a power-evolving universe, the world is upcoming, expanding, and becoming better with every passing day. Due to the appearance of negative circumstances, it may on the surface seem like there is a going backwards, but in a power-evolving universe, you will discover that going backwards is impossible. The negative circumstances are merely an appearance; and behind the appearances, there is a much greater good moving us onwards and upwards towards the goal of self-realisation, peace, and prosperity.

The universe cannot bare good for evil, or evil for good. Every positive thing has its negative polarity; they are two sides to the same coin and they both serve their purpose. All seemingly bad circumstances are necessary cogs in the upbringing and evolution of humanity. Without bad people, you wouldn't know who the good people were. Without being cold, you wouldn't know what it was like to be warm. Without getting sick, you would never know what it means to be well. Life is simply a series of lessons, and all situations are there to teach us, so that we may learn, so that we may grow. When humanity learns the lessons that each seemingly bad situation provides, they will fade away and a new lesson will take its place. Humans learn through two sources—through pleasure and pain. No one of the two is better or more desirable than the other; they both serve their purpose and without experiencing life through both of these sources, we wouldn't learn very much.

So, behold the universe is perfect and that nothing is out of place. We must learn to embrace our inadequacies, we must embrace the negatives as much as we embrace the positives, for these negatives are what also push us as a collective; and they are what gives us the drive to both thrive and become better. One of the laws of the universe is the law of polarity. That is to say that everything has its poles, you cannot have success without failure, good without evil, or righteousness without sin. Everything has its opposite and each thing is just as valid as to its counterpart. Indeed, every failure carries with it the seed of an equivalent advantage, and if we cannot appreciate the failure, how could we ever truly appreciate the success.

> "Things are as they are, looking out into the universe we make no comparisons between right and wrong stars, nor between well and badly arranged constellations."
>
> -Alan Watts

You now have at your disposal the knowledge needed for us to draw a close on Part I. We will now be moving on over to Part II where we will be clearing the mind so that you can successfully make use of the knowledge.

PART II: CLEARING THE MIND FOR SUCCESS

You have been introduced to the components of knowledge which you need, and you are almost ready to apply that knowledge to the attraction and maintenance of health. But before applying the knowledge to the aim of maintaining health, we first clear the mind of any unfavourable thought patterns, beliefs, doubts, and fears. Before any of this information can be put into successful use, the mind must be cultivated in a similar way to the plot of land that was mentioned in 'the analogy of the garden'. Before the body can attract and maintain health, the mind must first become favourable to its attraction and for health to meet you in a future contingency, the way must be cleared for it here, in the present.

In this part of the book, we are going to focus on clearing the mind for success. We are going to work on the four essentials as mentioned in Part I. We are going to reorganise any subconscious belief which will not serve you and we are going to eradicate any fears, doubts, and worries which you may have. And when I say eradicate, I mean absolutely obliterate them. We will not stop until your current doubts, worries, and fears become laughable. And to help with this, I would highly recommend that you re-read this part of the book at least three times before moving over to Part III. This isn't absolutely essential, but it is highly recommended. The importance of repetition when learning to apply these principles cannot be stressed enough. Internalisation is the foundation of succeeding in the use of this philosophy, and repetition is the foundation of internalisation itself.

Through repetition, you will change your way of thinking, which will, in turn, alter your perception. Your perception of the world will always be in direct proportion to the way the world presents itself to you. Your perception is responsible for what you see, how you think, and how you act. The lens from which you view the world is ultimately the cause of that which you experience. Remember, we don't see things as they are, we see things as we are, and if you begin to change the way you look at things, the things you look at will begin to change.

The universe is like a mirror and it provides you with a constant reflection that reflects how you currently view it, and how you feel about how you view it. Don't like the reflection? Then change your perception. The majority of the world experiences the things which they don't want to experience, and the reason why is simple. Firstly, because they predominantly think about the things that they don't want to happen and so, they create those things. And secondly, when those things arrive, they react in a negative way. But what you need to realise is that the reflection is always a step in front. The reflection of today is the result of your reaction to last month's reflection. And the reaction of today will be the cause of next month's reflection. So, when you react negatively to any situation, you are reacting to something you created a month ago, and in doing so, you will create a negative reflection for next month, which will more than likely cause yet another negative reaction. And so, the negative reflections never end. It's living in reaction to the reflection and it's a never-ending cycle because the reflection is creating their feelings, but they don't realise that their feelings are what creates the reflection. If you are in front of a mirror, for example, smiling with the biggest smile in the world, the reflection in the mirror is also smiling. But you are not smiling because the reflection is. The reflection is smiling because of you. If you change expression and frown, then the mirror will reflect it; reality works in a very similar way. So always choose to smile because if you frown, next month's reflection will give you something to frown about.

YOU CAN HAVE, DO, OR BE ANYTHING YOU WANT

You are more powerful than you know. You have within you the very same power which was used in creating the universe. Whether you are aware of this power or not, I know that you know deep down that there is something special about you. You know that somehow there is more to you than what meets the eye. You know without a doubt that within you, you have the ability to have, be, or do more than you currently do. Unconsciously, we all know this, and we knew this at birth. Coming into this world as a clean slate, we had no fears, no doubts, and no worries. It is only through social influence that we have picked these up and have created around ourselves the barriers to our infinite possibilities. At birth, we are pure and unrestricted by the confines of the collective consciousness. We are free from human expectancy and from the belief system contained within the collective consciousness. As we grew up, we were taught what was possible, what was not, what we could do, and what we couldn't. The commands happen repetitively throughout our childhood and eventually, we internalise these commands and accept them as truth. We tune into the vibrations of the collective, the vibrations of lack, fear, worry, and doubt. And because of this, we carry out our existence confined to these limitations. But the truth is, these limitations are self-imposed. You can have, do, or be whatever you want. Nothing is impossible for you. Anything your mind can conceive and believe, your mind can achieve.

Everything in your life, you have created. Every relationship, every material possession, every situation you have experienced was the result of the power of your creation. Through the workings of the mind and through the six mental faculties, you have tailor-made all your circumstances in life. Nothing has ever happened to you outside of your own awareness and nothing ever will. Without you being conscious, there is no experience. So, you need to understand that it is the power of this awareness which gives you the experiences of life. It is this power which creates them, and you can control this power, in fact, you do it all the time. If you weren't controlling this power, and if you weren't creating the experience of life, you would have been stuck at the first word in this sentence without the ability to move through to the last word of the sentence. You would be stuck at just one of the infinite points in time, without the ability to shift your consciousness from one point to the next.

"We are the painters of our own reality, and our attitude is the brush."

TIME AND SPACE

Time and space are both illusive; they are just tools which our minds use to navigate the physical plane. They are not an actual measurable structural fact. In other words, they are not laws. They are subjective because they are subject to interpretation. If this were not true, time would pass by the same for everybody and it would be impossible for time to be experienced differently from individual to individual. But this isn't the case. For example, let's imagine that Bill and Ben are playing tennis. Bill loves tennis, it's his favourite sport and he enjoys it. Ben, on the other hand, does not. He only goes along to please Bill and he really doesn't enjoy it at all. I think you would agree that time will go much faster for Bill than it would for Ben.

Another example: Debbie is talking to Anne about her day. She asks Anne how her day was to which she replies, "It has been a horrible day—everything seemed to go wrong and time just seemed to drag".

To this, Debbie responds, "Well, my day was wonderful. Everything seemed to go right, time just flew by". There is a reason why time flies on your day off but drags when you are at work and it's because of your perception of the activity. So this proves time itself is only a perception, for if it were a structural law or a mechanical fact, the experience simply could not differ from individual to individual or from activity to activity—it just wouldn't be possible. Regardless of how much fun you were having or how mundane the activity was, time would seem to go by in exactly the same uninterrupted way.

Every moment in time, every nanosecond is completely timeless. Life is a series of pictures, much like a movie. A movie is often referred to as a motion picture because it is a picture in motion. Life is very similar because every nanosecond is a picture that exists without time. And your life and the experience of time is simply the result of your consciousness flowing through the pictures and giving you the impression of a linear trajectory in order for you to experience change and to experience the effect of making decisions. Without this impression, you would be stuck at one particular point, one particular picture. You would essentially be lost in time.

There is an infinite number of pictures, all existing simultaneously, and there are infinite realities that exist for you. As the creator and chooser of your own reality, you transition your consciousness from one timeless nanosecond to the next timeless nanosecond. From one timeless picture to the next. There is an intelligence which does this subconsciously, and it is as effortless as the intelligence that subconsciously beats your heart because they are the same intelligence. It is the same intelligence that effortlessly keeps the earth spinning in perpetual motion, which effortlessly causes the sun to rise and the flowers to blossom. The intelligence which controls these is all one and the same. And you have this power within you. Now, I'm telling you all this to make you aware of one thing: that you are the creator of your own experience and that you subconsciously move your consciousness through the infinite number of timeless pictures from one picture to the next. You do this every nanosecond and have done so since birth. Now I need you to realise that you also have the power to consciously choose which pictures to transition your consciousness into. You have the power to only transition into the ones which you perceive as being 'good'.

This is why you can have, do, or be anything you want. This is why you are more powerful than you know. And this is why you need not have any fears, doubts, or worries, for if you knew of the true nature of your being, such emotions would be seen as preposterous.

"Time and space are both an illusion, just tools with which our conscious mind uses in order to navigate the manifestation."

THE SIX BASIC FEARS

The six basic human fears derive from a lack of understanding regarding just four questions: What am I? Why am I here? Where did I come from? Where am I going? With these questions answered, the emotions of fear, doubt, and worry will rapidly become obsolete. So, I am going to provide you with one of my essays entitled, 'The Unity of Creation', and it will answer these four questions for you, which will, in turn, stamp out the six basic fears once and for all. But first, I am going to explain how and why answering these four questions will make fear, doubt, and worry obsolete.

"Fear is simply a thought-form which has been projected into a future possibility. Fear is a misuse of imagination and it does nothing but remove you from the present moment."

The fear of poverty:

The fear of poverty will no longer be a concern for when you have the answers to these four questions because you will realise that poverty is only a mindset. You will realise that abundance is a mindset also, and it becomes quite evident that you have the power within you to tune into either of these states of mind. You will understand that you are not a victim of external circumstances but instead the conscious creator of them. This knowledge certainly dampens out the greatest fear of them all. If you can get rid of this fear, the other five fears will pack up and leave with it.

"Poverty is only a mindset."

- Napoleon Hill

The fear of criticism:

The fear of criticism will no longer be an issue, for you will be rooted firmly in your being to such an extent that you are no longer located on the competitive plane, but instead, you will be located in a place where criticism has no power—the creative plane. Only those in competition worry about criticism, creators, on the other hand, do not. You will begin to uncover the divine oneness of all creation and from this, you will associate all beings and situations as being simply an extension of self. When you are no longer identifying as a separate entity, the fear of being criticised is extinguished completely because it's only on the plane of duality where a 'separate' entity's criticism is seen as a form of judgment. However, on the plane of oneness, it is viewed as nothing more than feedback.

"Only those in competition fear criticism, creators, on the other hand, do not."

The fear of ill health:

The fear of ill health will have no effect because you will understand that disease has no real reality of its own. You will see that it is only an appearance and that the reality is health. Furthermore, you will understand that disease has its beginnings in thought. To think of disease produces the corresponding image of the disease in your own mind, which will ultimately produce the disease in your body. Knowing this and coupling it with the knowledge that you have been blessed with the ability to choose what to think, you realise that you have the ability to think of health and thus, create a corresponding image of health in your mind, and ultimately, produce health in your body. The word 'disease' derives from the words 'dis' and 'ease' when broken down. All forms of disease are caused by a body that it is not at ease. And with the ability to choose what to think, you can put your body at ease by thinking thoughts which correspond to the image which constitutes 'ease'.

"There is no disease, it is only an appearance. The reality is health."

- Wallace Wattles

The fear of loss of love:

The fear of loss of love will be nullified as you will embody the love of oneness and love of yourself. Any other love will simply serve as an addon, a perk or an extension to the already overflowing appreciation that you have for yourself. You will already feel complete and so your happiness will be generated by this feeling rather than by any external craving for completeness.

You will see that before entering the physical plane, you were whole. Upon arrival into this plane, the need for this wholeness, again, is what causes the feeling of incompleteness. You arrived as either man or woman, which is to say that you arrived as half of the whole. The search for this other half is the cause of frustration and dissatisfaction. Relying on finding the other half to complete you is counterproductive because not being whole is only an appearance, and the reality is that you are complete. No external person, situation, or material can complete you—and it never will. The only thing that can complete you is your understanding of your true nature, and that nature is oneness. When you realise this, you will no longer yearn or crave the love of another; you can enjoy the experience of another's love, but your happiness will no longer be dependent on it. And so, quite naturally, you learn to get on regardless of who enters or exits in your life. You will learn to get on with the love and completeness that comes with loving and appreciating yourself.

Most relationships fail because either one or both parties involved don't love themselves enough, and so they use their partner to fill that empty space. In doing so, there is always a giver, and there is always a taker. This ultimately leaves one's love meter completely drained, and the others love meter artificially full.

Relationships work when two people, who have a love for themselves above all else, get together. They don't rely on the love of the partner because their love meters are already overflowing, so rather than giving and taking, they share their overflowing love.

People with self-love have more than enough love for themselves to share with other people. And so, in the process of sharing it, nobody's love is being depleted and they can fill the other's meter without it impeding their own self-worth. The exchange is always unconditional and in the right proportion. If two people like this get together, it makes for a very happy relationship.

> *"You are complete, as you are. Another's love is only an add-on, not a necessity."*

The fear of old age

The fear of old age will be countered when you realise that age is an indication of experience. This fear makes very little sense because ageing will happen whether you want it to or not. It is, however, up to you how gracefully you age and whether or not you view it as a hindrance or an achievement. Old age is the accumulation of experience, wisdom, and knowledge. No one stage of life is better or worse than any other; they all play their part in the evolution and growth of your soul, and they all have their pros and cons.

The fear of old age is generally a fear that stems from the fear of the other basic fears. If one is old and poor, it can be a fearful prospect to struggle for food in a much weaker state. If one is old, he may feel he is unneeded and so, ultimately, is criticised or unappreciated. With old age can bring with it the fear of ill health because of the ageing body and its weaker immunity. Old age can bring a loss of sex appeal which potentially causes the fear of losing love. And with old age, it brings closer the fear of the unknown—the fear of death.

When you remove the previous fears as mentioned in the preceding paragraphs, the fear of old age will naturally be removed with them, providing you eradicate the last of the six fears which will be spoken about in the following paragraph. After nursing the other five fears, this fear will fade. Let us not forget, reaching old age is a blessing, denied to many. It should not be feared but rather, it should be the goal and a means of celebration if reached.

"Old age is a blessing, denied to many."

The fear of death:

The fear of death is by far the silliest of the six. Death will come. None of the other five fears is guaranteed, and so with them, it is the uncertainty of the possibility that is the cause for fear. But when it comes to the fear of death, it is the only thing that is guaranteed. It is the polar opposite of life. They are two sides to the same coin; if you fear life, you fear death. If you embrace life, naturally you will embrace death. This fear, of course, stems from the uncertainty of what lies beyond it. And the only way to surmount this fear is to understand the eternal nature of creation. When this is understood, the fear will be eradicated completely, for you will understand that your body is like a car, it is just a vessel, a vehicle which is used to navigate the physical plane. The driver is eternal and when the vehicle breaks down and is no longer viable for the job, the driver will simply get a new vehicle, one which works.

People who live fully for today seldom fear death, they are too involved in the act of living. It is only those who haven't lived fully or attempted to reach their full potential who fear death and it's because they know in their heart that if death stared them straight in their face, they would be riddled with regret. Human beings are not perfect, we all sin to some extent and we all know that we do, but that is why we are here. We are here to transcend our inadequacies and overcome them as a collective. Most people fear the prospect of being sent to a fiery hell to burn for eternity, and that is a scary prospect indeed. But you must realise, that is not where you are going. Heaven and hell are metaphors within religious scriptures to metaphorically outline that earth will become a living hell if you sin, and if you succumb to evil thoughts, you will attract an evil circumstance. Your life will be a misery because your soul yearns for advancement and so it impedes itself and its own evolution as a result. The likely case would be that you will have to retrace your steps over and over again until you get it right. If, however, you embrace love and you live in peace, you will attract loving peaceful circumstances to yourself. Your life here on earth will be as heavenly as the cloudy safe haven in which you imagine it to be up in the sky, and it is likely you will not have any steps to retrace because you will be in a vibration of progression, not regression.

If you begin to embrace life, you will quite naturally begin to embrace death. Know that all creation is eternal and as you will soon find out, what lies beyond is not as uncertain or as frightening as you have been made to believe. Death is merely transition; it is the transmuting of energy from one form into another. Furthermore, life is not something which happens to you, it happens for you. And so, because its polar opposite is death, this means that death, too, isn't something which happens to you, but rather something which happens for you.

> "Death will come to all, whether you embrace it or not. It's a necessary component of life."

Now, to help you make use of the knowledge listed above, and to aid in the removal of fears, doubts, and worries, I will now present to you one of my essays, 'The Unity of Creation'. Hopefully, by providing the answers to the four baffling questions of life, you will uncover the true nature of your being and in the process, become aware of the power that lies dormant within you, just waiting, to be called into action.

THE UNITY OF CREATION

What am I? Why am I here? Where did I come from? Where am I going? These are the questions which have plagued humanity since our arrival into the physical plane. These questions perplex all reason and induce a state of anxiety and fear in the minds of the many who are unable to deduce a logical explanation. I have found it to be my duty and of a complete necessity to shed a little light on the subject. To provide the world with an explanation, and one which is so desperately needed. But, before I do, I wish to explain the reasoning behind why the majority of the world is out of sync. Why the vast majority of the world's population lives in a state of fear and ignorance to the truth. A truth that lies in plain sight and can be seen with ease; if only our attentions were guided and directed in the right direction.

We live in a system that has been designed to keep us unaware of this truth. It has been purposely designed to keep us locked within our five senses with the sinister goal of preventing us the ability to transcend our awareness beyond what we can see, hear, smell, taste, and touch. Existence is a threefold unity; it consists of cause, it consists of law, and it consists of effect. To put this simply, there is an ultimate cause which, by making use of the law, generates an effect. The physical plane is the effect, the physical world in which we live and all of the atoms of matter that constitutes the physical world is the effect of a law, which operates in conjunction to the will of an ultimate cause.

The problem with the world today is that we have been taught to observe only the visible effect of things and we have not been taught to observe the invisible laws which govern the effect, or, to pay any attention to the unseen cause which makes use of the law. To be aware of only one part of this unity is bound to create confusion in any mind which tries to comprehend the nature of reality. To be aware of only one part of the unity and to neglect the other two which make up the whole, prevents one from seeing the full picture and thus, will not allow the truth to present itself. In Christianity, this threefold unity is referred to as the Holy Trinity. The father, the son and the holy ghost. The father is the cause, the son is the effect, and the holy ghost is the law. We will come back to this a little later.

Now, I wish to speak about why there is a sinister motive to keep people ignorant of the unity and what could be gained by doing so. There are a few people alive today who understand the workings of the universal laws and who possess a complete understanding of the unity and the components relative to its threefold nature. Due to knowledge acquired, which has been passed down and kept a secret through the centuries, these people are very aware of the stupendous amount of power that each one of us has in our possession. Quite simply, these people wish to keep you ignorant of this power. Their reason for doing so is that it gives them the opportunity to create the reality that they wish to create and that way, they can keep the power to themselves and dictate the unfolding of our advancement; ultimately, providing them with complete power and control.

To achieve this, they use various methods designed to induce fear and spread misinformation to the end of conquering the world through a subtle yet effective divide and conquer tactic. This is done namely through the sources of religion, politics, education, entertainment, and media. Through these sources, they attempt to control the minds of the masses. Through organised religion, they label and divide them; through politics, they govern and control them; through media, they distribute propaganda to misinform them; through entertainment, they distract them, and; through the education system, they neglect to teach essential information to indoctrinate them on what to think. The combining of these sources has the effect of colouring the lens of perception in such a way that it implements the hidden agenda

THE METAPHYSICAL WAY

that they wish to impose and enforces the quest for dominion of power and ultimate control.

Within you, there is a deep reservoir of untapped and infinite potential. We all possess an unfathomable amount of power; a power which can be described as nothing less than Godly. What is this power? Super strength? Invisibility? Time travel? No, the power you possess transcends all of these. If you imagine a super villain who possesses every superpower imaginable (telepathy, telekinesis, teleportation, invisibility, super speed, ultra-hearing, time travel, invincibility, etc.), then you may ask what one power could possibly make the strength of this villain obsolete? If he had every superpower imaginable, what one power could defeat him? That is the power of creation.

The power of creation is superior to all forms of power combined for it can create realities. With this power to create, a reality could be created where this villain has no power. A reality could be created where this villain's power no longer works. The creator can neutralise all efforts made by this super villain by making his efforts obsolete, or by creating a situation in which the villain no longer exists. You could, in theory, create whatever you desire. When you think of God, you don't imagine him as having teleportation powers or telepathy because his power transcends these. Instead, you call him the creator of reality, the creator of existence. This is the ultimate power, for what comes with it is the power to do everything else. And this is the power that you have at your disposal. As difficult as it may be to believe, you have in your possession the unrivalled power of creation. You are God's highest form of creation because you have been blessed with the mental faculties which allow for you to create and control your earthly destiny.

Man has the mental faculties necessary to create any reality which he can imagine. We have six enhanced mental faculties that separate us from the rest of the inhabitants of earth: imagination, intuition,

—— 63 ——

memory, perception, will, and reason. A dog can only make a mental picture of something that it has perceived through its five senses. When a dog dreams, it can only dream of that which it has experienced within the confines of its own physical experience. A human being, on the other hand, has been given the power of creative imagination. He can mentally picture that which does not currently exist as an actuality. He can picture situations, objects, and circumstances beyond the scope of his physical experience. He can dream of something which he has never even seen before. He doesn't have to have perceived it with his physical eyes; because as a human being, he has been given a third eye. He has been given a mind's eye and this is what we call the pineal gland. Through the pineal gland, he can use creative imagination to envision circumstances outside the scope of his physical reality and beyond the experiences in which he has been exposed to. This is the power of God, and the power of God is the power of creative imagination being willed into existence by using the law.

You have within you the very same power which God used in creating the universe. For, you have the power to creatively imagine, and the power of will to actualise that which you have imagined. If you doubt this to be true, it would be of benefit for us to resurrect Nikola Tesla so that we could ask him how he first creatively imagined, then secondly, willed the discovery of AC current, radio, x-ray, remote control, and the perfection of the modern incandescent light bulb into our physical existence. All of which were, at the time, outside the scope of his current physical reality. Steve Jobs imagined the iPhone before making it an actuality, and the iPhone could not have existed if he did not first form a mental image of it within his thoughts.

"Man can form things in his thoughts, and by impressing his thoughts upon formless substance, can produce the thing that is imaged by the thought". It won't be too long before science confirms that this 'formless' is, in fact, what we now refer to as 'dark matter'.

We think in pictures, and no material thing can be created without it first existing in the mind of man. The bridge you drive your car over is a real bridge. But before that bridge became real and before you could drive across it, it had to first exist as an idea in the mind of the man who visualised the bridge in all of its glorious details. This came before willing the command of action necessary to materialise that which he was visualising. The same applies to the car which is being driven over the bridge. "The kingdom of God is within you" because the power of God is within you. So then, what gives you this power of God? And what is God? The answer to both these questions? Consciousness.

Going back to the Holy Trinity, God is the father regarding the threefold unity of creation. And, the father is the cause. The cause is infinite. It is boundless. The cause is immeasurable. It has no beginning and it has no end—it simply just is. It always was, and it always will be. All philosophers, physicians, and theologists will agree on one thing, in spite of their differences, and that is that energy cannot be created or destroyed. It is eternal, universal, and infinite. It cannot be added to nor can it be subtracted from. Energy can only transmute from one form into another. Consciousness is pure energy. This energy is the uncaused cause of all that is. It is eternal, infinite awareness. And that is what you are. If you weren't conscious, you wouldn't be aware of your surroundings and you wouldn't be aware of this text.

Consciousness is not something which you have, it is something which you are. You are not a human being having a spiritual experience. You are a spiritual being having a human experience. Furthermore, you are not your body, or your mind. You are the consciousness which cooperates with the mind in order to utilise the body. You would never look at yourself in the mirror and affirm

'I am body' and it would be quite ridiculous as to say that 'I am mind'. You would, however, say, 'I am conscious'. And that, you most certainly are. Consciousness is the great 'I am'. And the great 'I am' is awareness—it is self-realisation. So, since God is consciousness, and since you are consciousness also, it is safe to say that not only do you have the power of God within you, but that, you are God. And that God is you. You are one in the same thing.

The brain is a sending and receiving station for the process of thought transmission, and it is the instrument which allows the mind to function. The mind operates in two parts; the conscious mind and the subconscious mind.

The conscious mind is the reasoning portion of the mind. It is the part which thinks it is the receiving station in the process of thought transmission. It receives thoughts through the sources of the five senses, infinite intelligence, and from the minds of other men. It receives them in the form of ideas, images, and plans through the faculty of the creative imagination. It is the part of the mind which wills, chooses, and makes decisions. The conscious mind is the chooser, it is self-aware, and it is intelligent. It is the word and the will of God. The conscious mind is the cause.

The subconscious mind is the subjective mind. It doesn't choose nor think. It simply just does. It is the subjective mind because it is subject to the will of the conscious mind. It responds to the will of the cause. The subconscious mind is the sending station in the process of thought transmission. Any thought which is repeated often enough and convincingly enough by the conscious mind is accepted and acted upon by the subconscious mind. Once the thought has been accepted as will, the subconscious mind will act and it will proceed to send the thought to infinite intelligence. Infinite intelligence is pure consciousness. It is the realm of infinite awareness. It connects to your conscious mind through the medium that is your subconscious mind. Pure consciousness is infinite. Your conscious mind is finite, but it is only finite in the sense that it is aware of only that which it experiences. It is, however, infinite in the sense that it can tune into the realm of the infinity. The subconscious mind is the medium through which this is accomplished. The subconscious mind is the law.

The cause and the law are co-existent. They are interdependent. In other words, the cause did not make the law; the law is co-eternal with the cause. The law is an attribute of the cause and they both exist together—they always have and they always will. They work in conjunction and in combination to generate the effect. The physical universe is the result of the cause working with the law. The physical universe is the effect.

Through the mental faculties of the mind, we can mould our environment. We can shape and create our circumstances of life. Man has been blessed with the control of just one thing—we can choose what we think. We cannot directly control our environment, but we can control our thoughts and so indirectly control our circumstances in life. Thought is an intangible impulse of energy and we can transmute that non-physical intangible impulse of energy into a tangible physical actuality. Thoughts are things, and they are very real. As Napoleon Hill once said, they are even more real than the brains in which the thoughts have been housed, because a thought has the power to live on even when the brain which has housed them has long turned to dust.

Thoughts are not something which our brains create. We do not create our thoughts, none of us do. We pick them out and we tune into the thoughts that already exist. Thoughts are impulses of energy; they exist in the realm of pure consciousness; the realm of infinite awareness. Energy cannot be created or destroyed, and so we cannot create our thoughts, but we can—and we do—tune into them. The brain is a sending and receiving station for the process of thought transmission. When you attempt to draw on a memory, you do not re-create that memory. The memory already exists, it always has and it always will. You tune into the memory with the will and the desire to tune into it, and through the aid of your subconscious mind, you bring that thought to the surface of your conscious mind. The same is true when drawing to your conscious mind a past memory as it is for drawing a future possibility.

Steve Jobs didn't create the thought which was necessary to create the iPhone. He tuned into the frequency of the thought which was necessary to create the iPhone. A caveman could have tuned in to the same frequency of thought which Steve Jobs did. The only difference between the caveman and Steve Jobs is that firstly, Steve Jobs formed a mental picture of it and tuned in to the desire to create it, whereas the caveman didn't. (And that is quite understandable. For, to tune into a desire of such magnitude before tuning in to the desire for clothes is quite absurd). And secondly, he mixed that desire with the emotion of faith and he believed that it could be done. His desire was given feeling through emotionalization, and through the will of his conscious mind, it was passed on to his subconscious mind. Any thought which is repeated often enough, and convincingly enough, is finally accepted. His subconscious mind tuned in to the thought vibrations of the infinite, which proceeded to send back the like thoughts, images, ideas, and plans of a similar vibration to the thought which was sent to it. His conscious mind received these thoughts through the faculty of the creative imagination, and he acted on these thoughts with persistence until the iPhone manifested.

It is quite likely that some form of aircraft appeared in man's mind hundreds of years ago. That doesn't mean he created the image of the aeroplane or the thought which constitutes the image. He tuned into the image. But that's as far as it went. The Wright brothers, on the other hand, they emotionalized the image and they mixed the desire for its realisation with the faith that it could become. And so, for them, it didn't remain a dream. It became an actuality. An artist always creates twice. First, he dreams of his painting. Then, he paints his dream.

Our reality is literally the outward physical expression of our inward non-physical impression of thought. Everything in the physical plane is illusive. It is a tangible manifestation of the intangible energy of awareness. The only true reality that exists, the only real actuality is energy. And, "If you wish to understand the universe, think in terms of energy, frequency, and vibration." For all matter is merely energy condensed and vibrating to a specific frequency. The material world, and all the atoms and molecules which make up the material world, are the effect of the cause working in cooperation with the law.

There is only one true substance. One true actuality. One intelligence. And, that is consciousness. Intelligence is the only true thing which exists. Everything else is just a manifestation of that intelligence and the laws which the intelligence uses to govern the manifestation. Time and space are both illusory; they are simply attributes of the effect, just tools with which we make use of in order to experience the effect. There is no such thing as duality, just the one true infinite point of awareness. This intelligence, this infinite point of awareness, manifests itself into the seemingly many elements which make up the universe. You were created in God's image because you are the image of the effect of God. And, we are not separate you and I, for as Bill Hicks once said, "We are all one consciousness experiencing itself subjectively, there is no such thing as death, because life is just a dream and we are the imagination of ourselves.

Now, to answer the questions to which this essay began.

What am I? You are the one consciousness manifesting itself into the seemingly many elements which make up the universe. You are a non-physical spiritual being having a physical human experience. You are energy in motion, being divinely guided by its infinite intelligence. You are not your body or your mind. Your body is just the effect. You are the one consciousness back of that effect. You are not your mind; for your mind is simply the law, the tool which the one consciousness uses to manifest the effect. You are the cause. The uncaused cause which always has been, always is, and always will be.

Why am I here? You are here to grow spiritually and to transcend your awareness beyond the limitations of the physical plane. You are here for self-realisation and to discover the true nature of your being. You are here to choose, to express, and to experience the joy that comes with the expression of free will through subjective creation.

Where did I come from? Where am I going? Time and space are both an illusion; all duality is. There is nowhere to come from and there is nowhere to go to. You never arrived and you never left. You are where you always are. Where you always were. And where you always will be. The only place that exists. The only place that has existed and the only place that will exist. At home, where you belong. In the realm of infinite awareness.

YOU NOW HAVE THE ANSWERS

It's a strange thing, life, but it's even stranger that the majority of people are perplexed by it. The answers to life's big questions are riddled in the way nature presents herself and in the observation of the universal laws. It just takes a still mind and a watchful eye, and all the answers jump out at you. Be still and pay close attention, then a new world of opportunity will be opened to you.

You have now been exposed to the answers which the majority of the world seeks, you have been given a glimpse into some of the universal laws and we have touched upon the true nature of your being. Therefore, you now have in your possession an adequate understanding and one which transcends the understanding possessed by the majority of the world. This alone should be sufficient enough to remove at least a modicum amount of fear, doubt, and worry.

Remember this, the creator is always more powerful than his creation. It can be no other way. There is no external situation that has the slightest power to defeat you because you create the situation. So, never permit yourself to become a victim of circumstance, you are not a victim; you are the creator of circumstance and the chooser of your own earthly experience.

Your environment is your reflection, it is a product of you. But, if you fail to take control of your environment, and if you live in reaction to it, then it will generate an unnecessary power; your environment will take on your role as creator and you will become a product of that environment.

> "Man is the creator of his own earthly destiny; he is the maker and shaper of his circumstances of life."

SUGGESTION

People can be made sick through negative suggestion, whether it be self-suggestion or suggestion given by another. Self-suggestion is by far more dangerous because self-suggesting indicates that you believe it to be true, usually. Even if you do not believe it, and even if the suggestion is simply a joke or a bid for some form of sympathy, it is a dangerous thing because your subconscious mind cannot differentiate between a joke and a truth. Your subconscious mind doesn't understand humour and it certainly doesn't offer any sympathy. If said with emotion, self-suggesting phrases such as "I feel like crap today" will be interpreted as truth and your subconscious will seek to present to you more circumstances which make you "feel like crap today". Remember, your subconscious mind doesn't know that you don't want to feel like crap; it only responds to what commands you give it, and it has no opinion. If you are speaking with a friend and you say jokingly, "I hope I don't get the virus", your subconscious mind will not register the word 'don't' in the way that your conscious mind does. Your subconscious mind will register it as a negative connector word, and by combining it to a negative power word (i.e. 'virus'), the whole suggestion becomes negative. The whole sentence is negative because 'I hope' shows a lack of certainty and powerlessness. Combining that to a negative connector, one which indicates that you 'do not want' something, and then further tying it to a power word such as 'virus', is a recipe for disaster. You have basically given away your power, and you have asked for exactly the thing which you don't want to happen. These day to day suggestions happen very frequently.

If you begin to watch your thoughts and your tongue in conversation, you will be amazed by the prevalence of these self-defeating suggestions. Whenever you notice a negative suggestion pop up or come out of your mouth, quickly cancel it out by replacing it with a positive one. Using the example given above, instead of "I hope I don't get the virus", say "I want to stay healthy". The difference between these two suggestions may seem minuscule, but that couldn't be further from the truth. It is a subtle change but the change is one which can have a ginormous effect, either for or against you. A lot of hypochondriacs eventually develop the disease in which they so commonly speak about. They have developed the habit of speaking about imaginary illness, usually with the goal of getting sympathy or as a means of avoiding work. They repeat these suggestions, so much that in the end, the imaginary illness manifests as an actual affliction.

You can be suggested to be sick by another individual. If another suggests sickness to you it doesn't necessarily mean you believe it and so it can often be disregarded. However, it all comes down to your level of susceptibility. For example, imagine a man sat next to you on a boat. This man doesn't like boats, they make him feel extremely anxious. You, as a joke, turn to this man and you tell him, "You look pale, it looks like you are going to be seasick". The man's susceptibility to this suggestion is very high, considering he doesn't like being on a boat. Ultimately, the man will believe what is being suggested and he will begin to feel seasick and look pale as a result. Now if you were to say exactly the same thing to the experienced captain who steers boats all day every day, then the suggestion would have no effect. He would very likely laugh in amusement to the absurdity of the suggestion. His conscious mind couldn't accept it as being true; it disregarded it completely and so the suggestion never made it through to the subconscious mind. The captain had a very low susceptibility to this suggestion.

Now imagine the same two characters, the passenger and the captain, but this time suppose the passenger had eaten 10 sandwiches and you suggested to him that he must be hungry, the suggestion would likely be disregarded. Now if you suggested the same thing to the captain who, being busy at work hadn't noticed that he hadn't eaten, then the suggestion will likely be accepted and passed onto his subconscious mind which would then begin to make him suddenly aware of his hunger, potentially causing his stomach to rumble as a result. Suggestion is a very powerful thing. It can be likened to a painkiller; it will alleviate pain if used correctly but if used wrongly, it can result in misfortune and even death.

Suggestion is the reason why hypnotism works. Hypnotists basically lower brain wave activity to lower the guard of the conscious mind and thus, leaving the subconscious mind susceptible to suggestion. Once a hypnotist makes it past the conscious mind into the subconscious mind, suggestions can be planted whereby the 'subject' will now respond in alignment to that which was suggested. Suggestion is also what indirectly gives power to the phenomenon known as the 'placebo effect'. The placebo effect is where a subject is given a 'fake' pill such as a sugar pill with no medicinal benefits of any sort. The sugar pill is given in place of the medicinal pill to cure an illness or minor ailment. The subject, however, is not aware that it is a sugar pill because through suggestion he is made to believe that what he has taken is the real thing. This suggestion aroused the individual's emotion of faith which, in turn, healed the appearance of disease. It healed the illness in the exact same way that the real pill would have healed him. In fact, placebo often works better if done correctly as there are no negative side effects. Furthermore, the power of suggestion can break the placebo effect if the subject is later made aware of the trickery.

The placebo effect proves three truths. Firstly, it proves that suggestion can induce the emotion of faith. Secondly, that thought combined with the emotion of faith can heal the body and lastly, it demonstrates that thought without faith can nullify. The placebo effect is everywhere and in many areas of our life. In fact, our whole life is a placebo effect. But that is a whole other topic within itself. The point is that suggestion has immense power, and either you programme your subconscious mind yourself or somebody else will programme it for you. Your health, wellbeing, and liveliness are up to you. It is not down to any external, whether it be a person or situation. You have the ability to control what suggestions you accept and what suggestions you reject. You have the power to self-suggest anything you want your subconscious mind to accept. It is you alone who dictates the state of your health and it is you alone who has the power to maintain it.

"Every human being is the author of his own health or disease."

– Buddha

AFFIRMATIONS

Now, I wish to speak about affirmations. Affirmations are the deliberate use of autosuggestion. They are commands which you consciously affirm, commands which your conscious mind gives to your subconscious mind with the goal of having the subconscious mind accept the commands as truth so that it will act upon them. Remember, any thought which is repeated often enough and convincingly enough is finally accepted. The affirmations do not need to be true at the time because your subconscious mind cannot differentiate between truth and untruth. It will act on any thought which has been emotionalized and repeated often. If you tell yourself a lie over and over again, you will eventually bring yourself to accept that lie as truth. When you accept something as truth, the subconscious mind will accept it also.

Autosuggestion works in your favour if used correctly, if used wrongly it will work against you. Your subconscious mind does not care if the accepted truth is good for you or if it's bad. It will return what you put into it, but it is impartial, unemotional, and it has no opinion. If you are at a McDonald's drive-through and you ask for fries, the cashier will give you fries. It is of no concern to her whether you like fries or not; she doesn't ask whether or not you have diabetes, she simply responds to your request. The subconscious mind works in the same way. It will give you what you ask for and what you believe in—nothing more and nothing less. Affirmations are a useful tool to deliberately direct what the subconscious mind is fed through the aid of autosuggestion. On a daily basis, we are prone to wrongly using autosuggestion as we unconsciously feed our subconscious mind negative and unfavourable material. Affirmations can be used to counter this; they can serve as the cornerstone of your belief system and through constant repetition and emotionalization, they can cancel out any negative suggestions which you may have permitted to creep into your mind throughout the day.

Always start your affirmations with 'I am'. The words 'I am' are two of the most powerful words in the human language; it doesn't matter the dialect or culture. Whatever you put behind these words becomes your reality. Affirmations should always be presented in the present tense, for your subconscious mind has no comprehension of past recollections or future contingencies. It only knows now. To speak in past and future tense only affirms that you do not have what you are affirming here in the present, and so it rejects the affirmation. There is one exception to this rule, and that is you can affirm in future tense providing your affirmation is affirmed with a definite time and date. For example, a present-tense affirmation would be "I am so happy and grateful now that I am healthy". A present-future tense affirmation would be "I am healthy on 9th February 2021 at 3:00 PM". The latter of the two is more a way of instilling a goal with a deadline, but it is still an affirmation none the less. It is a way of affirming that a certain condition is there on a certain date. The reason it works in this instance is because of its definiteness and it doesn't imply that you are not healthy right now. Your subconscious mind doesn't know that the date is in the future—your conscious mind does. So, as long as you consciously believe that the date will be a date of health, your subconscious mind will believe it also. Just be sure it is affirmed with definite purpose, emotionalization, and repetition.

You must always affirm in the positive. Don't give credence to that which you don't want. For example, let us assume you want to be free from disease, let us assume that you want health. Your affirmation should not be "I am now free from disease". Your affirmation should be "I am now healthy" or "I am now full of health". Remember, to think of disease produces the corresponding image of disease in your own mind; we think in pictures and what you think about, you bring about. The subconscious mind doesn't hear the words 'free from'; those words are not what creates the image in your mind. Your subconscious mind does, however, hear the word 'disease' and the word 'disease' will create the image in your mind. In the two examples above, the words 'health' and 'disease' are the power words. The words 'full of' and 'free from' are simply connectors. Connectors are useful in affirmations, but only if they connect to a positive power word. If they connect to a negative word, they are nullified. A positive and a negative will cancel out the affirmation. A positive connector, connecting to a positive power word is a double positive, and it has a much greater effect. And if you attach a negative connector to a negative power word, well, that's just silly. Don't ever do that. The double negative will fly from your mind and it will come right back around to kick you in the bum.

I am now going to give you a list of affirmations to use. The first list is a compilation created by Justin Perry from 'You Are Creators' (be sure to visit his YouTube channel as it has an abundance of useful information). These affirmations cover all areas, and I myself use them daily. I will also add a separate section, specifically for the area of health. Repeat these affirmations as often as possible, internalise them and feel them to be true. Eventually, they will seep into your subconscious mind, you will accept them as belief, and they will then become a part of your inner dialogue. As a result, the positive, internal thoughts will soon manifest into a positive, external circumstance.

General Affirmations:

I am healthy	*I am wealthy*
I am wise	*I am brilliant*
I am magnificent	*I am genius*
I am exuberant	*I am happy*
I am cheerful	*I am joyful*
I am overjoyed	*I am strong*
I am powerful	*I am tenacious*
I am successful	*I am fortunate*
I am expansion	*I am rich*
I am wealthy	*I am affluent*
I am abundant	*I am bountiful*
I am prosperous	*I am healthy*
I am lively	*I am energetic*
I am honourable	*I am honest*
I am integrity	*I am courageous*

I am daring

I am educated

I am wise

I am discerning

I am a multi-millionaire

I am opulence

I am charitable

I am a piece of the creator

I am connected to the Source

I am boundless

I am wonderful

I am magnificent

I am a brilliant communicator

I am an overachiever

I am a goal-getter

I am a wonderful leader

I am charming

I am a pleasure to be around

I am broad intelligence

I am wise counsel

I am producing endless joy life

I am intrepid

I am prudent

I am business savvy

I am cunning

I am financially prosperous

I am generous

I am a philanthropist

I am a part of God

I am infinite

I am immeasurable

I am impressive

I am a magnificent speaker

I am a master at speech

I am outstanding

I am a massive success

I am a walking brilliance

I am charismatic

I am infinite wisdom

I am total understanding

I am creating more prosperity

I am now creating a magnificent

These affirmations are a perfect way for you to affirm and remind yourself of what you really are. By default, you are all of the above. Not a single affirmation listed is an inaccurate representation of the true nature of your being. Not a single one. Some of them may seem disagreeable to you right now, but that is only a misconception. The misconception arises as a result of the world getting its hands on you. But you were born unblemished, and you can become aware of your unblemished state once again. You are inconceivably limitless. You are literally immeasurable. The very essence of your being is downright unfathomable. I need you to understand that, and I need you to believe it. The more you repeat these affirmations, the more you will begin to accept them as truth. Any thought repeated often enough and convincingly enough is finally accepted. So, repeat them often, repeat them in a spirit of belief, and eventually, they will become a part of your subconscious beliefs. Once the truth has been accepted, the truth shall, without a doubt, set you free.

"A person's entire life is simply a collection of their affirmations."

THE FOUR ESSENTIALS

What we will cover now are the four essentials as mentioned in Part I. The four essentials were as follows: Desire, Faith, Gratitude, and Efficient Action. With the knowledge you have obtained, and with the removal of fear, we are now set to work on these four essentials to speed up the process of manifesting the circumstances of life that you want.

Desire

Desire is the starting point of all manifestation. A desire is an intangible impulse of energy, and it is what sets the wheels in motion on the road to manifestation. It serves as the major driving force for action because desire is the creator of feeling, and feeling is the cause of action. The goal is to intensify your desire to such an extent that your attention is focused on that desire constantly. When your attention is focused intensely upon your desire, it does two things:

Firstly, it prevents your mind from drifting. Drifting can be described as allowing your attention to stray from the thought-form which constitutes the image of your desire. The world is full of distractions and more often than not, these distractions do not serve you. TV, social media, other people etc., they all divert your attention; and energy flows where attention goes. You want your energy to flow to your desire, and you want it to flow there as much as practically possible. You want all doors closed tightly against any influences which don't aid in the desire's realisation. Every time you focus upon your desire, you kindle in your mind a build-up of energy towards it. The longer you focus upon it, and the greater the intensity of the focus, the more the energy expands. The more the energy expands, the greater the feeling which arises as a result. The greater the feeling, the greater the urge to act. Those actions will develop habits which are in alignment with the attraction of that which you desire. Habits are simply energy patterns. This energy pattern is what attracts the circumstance which resonates with the desire. Quite simply because it was the desire which indirectly caused the energy pattern.

Secondly, it helps in the generation of the other three essentials. When your mind is focused intensely on your desire, it allows no room for negative outside influences to creep in and discourage you. When your attention is laser-like, it remains focused on what you want, and no attention is paid to discouragement or negative suggestion. This lack of negative suggestion will eventually begin to inspire the emotion of faith. Due to the intense focus and the generation of faith, your vibration of thought will increase, and your frequency will rise as a result. Operating from this new level of frequency brings with it a new level of awareness, which, in turn, allows for an efficiency of action that wouldn't have been available to you on the lower plane. The efficiency of action inspires yet even more faith, resulting in the development of an attitude of gratitude which arises in response to the positive frequency, and in the realisation that progress is being made.

Desire is the most important of the four essentials because, without desire, faith, efficient action, and gratitude have but little use. Without a desire, why would you need faith? Why would you need to act? And what would you have to be grateful for? The importance of having an intense desire at all times cannot be stressed enough. Albert Einstein once said, "If you wish to find happiness, tie it to a goal, not people or objects". Desires and goals are very similar by nature. Desire is the driving force to all achievement and manifestation whether it be a desire to have, a desire to do, or a desire to become. It is the inducer of feeling, the main source for action. It is the creator of habit and the indirect shaper of circumstance. Man, without an intense desire, is like a plane without an elevator; no direction and no guidance system. He glides through life blindly without any control over his destination. The likely case being that he eventually runs out of fuel and crashes nose-first into a mountain of dissatisfaction.

To intensify your desire, first, you have to know exactly what your desire is—that goes without saying. But the most important thing is to become extremely clear about the reason why you want the desire to be realised. In other words, you need to give your desire a purpose. The purpose is what generates the act of persistence. It keeps your attention focused on the desire tenaciously and it is what keeps your mind closed to external suggestion. A desire in of itself is simply an impulse of energy, but that energy has no power unless it is given a direction. The purpose is what will give the energy a direction.

To intensify your purpose, visualise. Use creative visualisation to picture the attainment of your purpose. See the attainment of your purpose as being already accomplished and while doing so, feel the feelings which come with its attainment. The goal of the visualisation is to induce positive feelings. To induce these feelings, picture the image clearly, down to its finest detail, and make the image as real as possible in your mind. To make the image clear, use your senses to see the image, hear the image, smell the image, taste the image, and feel the image. The image, and the feeling which arises from the image, is to serve as a trigger for when your mind begins to drift. If done correctly, the reality of the trigger and the positivity of the feeling associated with it will bring your mind right back to where it needs to be. To increase the power of the feeling, you can attach to the image a feeling which occurred in your past; one which you remember as being extremely positive. Tie this feeling into the visualisation. Then, if your mind ever does begin to drift, simply picture the image, and then the feeling which was tied to it will arise in conjunction with the image. The ultimate goal is to never allow this image and the feeling to fade—you want to hold the image with unwavering consistency. After a while, the image will hold itself, it will become fixated in your mind and it will eventually impel subconscious action towards its attainment.

As you visualise, close your eyes. Then roll them slightly upwards as if trying to look at your forehead. Now, breathe deeply, in through your nose for four Mississippi's, then out through your mouth for four Mississippi's. Concentrate on your breathing. As you do this, see your visualisation vividly, feel it deeply, and believe it to be yours for the taking. If you do this in a spirit of faith, it soon will be.

> "Desire is the starting point to all achievement."
>
> -Napoleon Hill

Faith

To believe that the reality is being given to you, you must cultivate the emotion of faith. Faith is the strongest of the positive human emotions, and when it comes to manifesting an intangible desire into the physical plane, it is by far the most efficient. There really is no substitute. With this being said, faith is also quite often the most difficult emotion to cultivate because it's polar opposite is fear; and most people fail to shake off the negative emotion of fear in their lifetime. The law of polarity is one of the 12 universal laws. This law dictates that everything has its poles, everything has its opposites. That is to say that black has it's white, up has it's down, left has its right, north has its south. You cannot be positive and negative at the same time in the same way that you cannot be both tall and short. Likewise, you cannot embody the emotion of faith while you embody the emotion of fear. Being polar opposites, where one persists the other cannot remain. One of the two must dominate.

Since the system is designed in such a way that it promotes negativity, and since the collective consciousness is currently operating in a state of fear, fear frequencies are naturally picked up and so faith is rarely present in the minds of individuals. Which is unfortunate because the immense power of faith cannot be emphasised enough. The emotion of faith can key up the vibrations of thought to such an extent that it instantaneously creates a direct path to source energy. This then proceeds to produce the reality that is in conjunction with the impulse of thought, with which the emotion of faith was mixed.

Faith has healing power, there are many instances where individuals have attended a faith healing and have been completely healed. There are many artefacts all over the globe which are said to possess healing power. People travel around the world to visit these healing artefacts and a lot of the time, healing takes place. The healing is dependent on the individual's faith in the artefacts' healing powers. The artefact has no power of its own, but the faith in the artefact is what gives the artefact its apparent power. Superstition is nothing more than negatively applied faith, by which I mean an individual hands their power of faith to an external object, being, or situation. One might say that he has a 'lucky' coin, for example, or he may say that it is 'bad luck' to smash a mirror. The truth is, the coin isn't lucky at all, and it is not bad luck to smash a mirror. But it is our thinking and our faith in the superstition which makes it so. Without superstition, it is just a coin. Without superstition, it is just a broken mirror. And when you attach faith to the thought pattern regarding the superstition, then it is likely that the coin will bring you some 'luck' and it is likely that the broken mirror will bring you some 'bad luck'. Faith creates expectation, and expectation is what attracts to you the circumstance that aligns with that which you expect.

There was a case not too long ago where a homeless man was laying on some cardboard fast asleep. A couple of teenagers walked by the man and being armed with a paintball gun, they thought it would be amusing to open fire on the poor fellow. They let three shots off and ran away. The man awoke from his sleep, he looked down at his chest, saw the red paint, and collapsed momentarily. He lost consciousness and he didn't regain it. This death was down to fear which induced shock. This man quite simply expected to die, and so he did. The fact that fear can kill a man goes to show that faith, the polar opposite of fear, can heal one.

On the paragraph on suggestion, we spoke about the placebo effect. The placebo effect only works because the one who is subject to the placebo has faith in the pill which he is taking. After receiving the suggestion, his conscious mind blends faith with the suggestion and so it instantly reaches his subconscious mind. The subconscious mind proceeds to produce the result which resonates with the faithful thought that was passed to it. When a subject is told the truth that the pill has no medicinal properties, he loses faith in the pill and so the healing is neutralised.

Faith can be cultivated in multiple ways. But the main avenue for the cultivation of faith is through understanding. When you begin to understand the nature of reality and the workings of the universal laws, faith arises automatically as a result. This is because, through understanding, fear is eliminated. When fear is eliminated, there is only one thing that can take its place; that is the emotion of faith. So, to inspire faith in your own mind, you must begin to see the truth behind all things. You must begin to understand the nature of reality and how it functions. You need to understand your true nature and you need to understand the true nature of nature itself. For when you do gain this understanding, you will gain a higher level of awareness. A high level of awareness naturally encourages the emotion of faith, and it discourages the emotion of fear. All the understanding that you need has been presented to you in this book. The main understandings to consider are:

1) You have complete control over "The workings of the mind".

2) You are a creative power, "You can have, be, or do whatever you want to".

3) The universe is exactly how it is meant to be. "It is all part of the divine plan".

4) The universe is threefold in its "Unity of Creation".

A thorough understanding of "The Unity of Creation" should be sufficient enough in the cultivation of faith because if you grasp the message conveyed, the answers to the four questions within will eliminate "The six basic human fears" and quite naturally, faith will cultivate itself as a result.

The second way to cultivate faith is through the use of autosuggestion, which is covered in "The workings of the mind". Remember, any thought repeated often enough and convincingly enough is finally accepted by the subconscious mind. You can cultivate faith by telling yourself that you have faith. If you affirm to yourself that you have faith and if you emotionalise the affirmation over and over again, you will eventually begin to believe it, and so, your subconscious mind will act on that belief by actualising that which you believe. Below is an affirmation which you can use. If you repeat this affirmation, you will gradually begin to cultivate the emotion of faith:

"I am increasing my faith every day. I have faith in myself and I have faith in the universe. I can have, be, or do whatever I want to, and the universe is exactly the way it is meant to be."

The third and final way to cultivate faith is through gratitude. Quite simply because a grateful mind is a deserving mind; a deserving mind will expect the best and expectancy leads to faith. To learn how to develop the attitude of gratitude, we will move over to the third essential.

"If thoust can believe, all things are possible to him that believeth."

- Mark [9:23]

Gratitude

Gratitude brings your mind into harmony with source energy because gratitude is appreciation, and appreciation is the language of creation. Creation occurs so that it can be appreciated. The cause manifests the effect so that it can appreciate and marvel in its own intelligence and beauty. In the same way a human being wants to be valued, a flower wants to display its beautiful colours; a star wants to shine brightly; lightning wants to flash to be seen; thunder wants to be heard; lions want to be respected; trees want to beautify the land; the vastness of seas want to amaze; the sound of the waves want to calm; fruits and vegetables want to appeal. Creation is by its very nature, seeking appreciation. Gratitude puts you directly in alignment with the purpose of life; it causes you to see the good in everything and, consequently, everything begins to see the good in you. Not only does it generate faith, but gratitude also makes you a better person. And the whole world will soften towards you because of it.

To cultivate an attitude of gratitude, appreciate. Simply use autosuggestion to affirm to yourself all the things which you are grateful for. List things such as family, friends, food, your divine relationship to the universe, being alive, having the opportunity to grow, clean water, clothes, health, possessions—basically all the things which are usually taken for granted. The best thing to be grateful for, and by far the most powerful, is to be grateful for being here in the now. If you can learn to appreciate the moment of now without constantly dwelling on the past or projecting your thoughts out into the future, then you have learnt to be grateful for the only thing there ever is, the only thing there ever was, and the only thing there ever will be. You will have learnt to appreciate the gift of life, and that's why it's called the present.

Below is an affirmation to induce an attitude of gratitude:

"I am so grateful to be alive and well. I am thankful for every moment that I am blessed with and I am grateful for every opportunity that those moments provide."

"You cannot exercise much power without gratitude, for it is gratitude that keeps you connected with power."

- Wallace Wattles

Efficient action

Action, it's the word that scares away the would-be conscious creator. When people first hear about the law of attraction, they believe that the law of attraction will bring to them the things that they want without them ever having to do anything; without ever putting in some form of action. This is not the case. Those with only a misty concept of the law wrongly assume that all they have to do is visualise. They pick up on the notion of "ask, believe, and receive" but they don't realise that, although that process is very true, it is also very simplified. It should actually be stated as "ask, believe, act-receive". But I assume the teachers of the law of attraction left that part out because the lazy nature of a human being will see that as a deterrent. Although it shouldn't serve as a deterrent because to act does not mean to work hard, not in the slightest.

To ask, is to form the image of your desire. To believe, is to bring it towards you. To act, is to provide for its reception and, to receive, is to obtain it. Once the image has been created, whatever constitutes the image has been created also, it now exists. Once you believe that it is already yours, you charge the reality of the image with energy and it begins to move towards you. Through action, you provide for the reception of the thing you want, and by action, you receive it. This is where 99% of people who fail to receive go wrong. They create the image, but they fail to take it any further. These people are known as 'castle builders' because they build but they don't receive. Even if they take it to the next step and they believe it to be theirs, they may begin to pull the reality towards them but they fail to meet the reality by acting in a certain way.

Jim Carrey once said, "You can't just visualise and then go and make a sandwich". And that is very true, unless, of course, you are visualising being a chef. One which specialises in making sandwiches. What Jim Carrey meant by this was that you cannot just visualise and sit back—

you must provide for the reception of the visualisation by acting upon it. If we refer back to the analogy of the bridge mentioned in 'The Unity of Creation', you can really see the truth in this. "The bridge is a real bridge, but before it became real it first existed in the mind of the man who visualised the bridge in all of its glorious details. This came before willing the command of action necessary to materialise that which he was visualising". The man didn't just hold the image of the bridge in his mind and stop at that. He first asked for the bridge by picturing in his mind the type of bridge, and he pictured this down to its finest detail. He then believed the bridge would be made and so, his belief brought to him the men, the resources, and everything else that was necessary for creating the bridge. Lastly, he acted by organising the men, the resources, and setting them to work on the building of the bridge. Upon completion, he received that which he asked for in his mind.

In the Bible, there is a story in 2 king's chapter 3:16-19 which outlines how faith and action combined will get you what you want. In this story, the armies of Israel, Judah, and Edom were stuck in the hot desert and dying of thirst. The kings went to the prophet Elijah and asked for a word from God. Elijah told them as follows, "Dig ditches all over this valley. You won't hear the wind, you won't see the rain, but this valley is going to fill up with water and your army and your animals will drink their fill. The kings didn't quite understand, "It never rains here, and there is a drought" they said confusingly. Elijah replied, "If you want to see rain, you have to dig the ditches first." So, they dug the ditches, and the next day, the ditches were filled to overflowing. The drought had ended.

When you ask the universe for something, you must prepare for the reception of that thing by putting in the necessary action. You must combine action with faith, by acting in full confidence and with utmost certainty, that the thing you have asked for will arrive. By asking, you create. By believing, you bring it to you. And, by action, you receive. The reason action is so important is because, by acting, it demonstrates to the universe and to yourself that you have faith. You see, anybody can hold an image in their mind while they affirm that they have faith, but only he who provides for the reception of the image by acting on it, actually demonstrates faith. Faith without action is dead. Quite simply because faith needs a channel to present itself, and it just so happens that action is that channel.

The universe itself is in constant action, everything is energy, in a rhythmic motion. All things vibrate, nothing rests. Everything ebbs and flows. The universe will not stand idle, that is why it is forever in the act of creating things. It likes immediate decisive action backed by faith, and it rewards it. It doesn't reward procrastination, for procrastination goes against the very nature of the unfolding of advancement; procrastination goes against faith. Those who get ahead in life are those who act, not those who wait for the right time to act. In waiting for the right time, the right time will never come and the opportunity you are waiting for will keep on passing you by.

It all comes down to the 'five-step process' again whereby, thought is asking, feeling is believing, action is receptiveness, habit is persistence, and circumstance is receiving. If we look back at the analogy of the garden again, you will see that your actions are the water. If you don't water the crop, you will not receive the plant. If you don't act on the image, you will not receive the reality.

Once you have formed your mental picture, and have given thanks for it, you must act, and you must act now. You cannot act tomorrow, for there is no tomorrow. By the time tomorrow comes around it is once again, now. You must not wait for the right conditions to act, for if you do, those conditions will never arrive. The conditions you are waiting for will arrive through your actions in the present, so it is important to act now, whether you feel ready to act or not.

THE METAPHYSICAL WAY

The importance of acting from where you are cannot be stressed enough—you can only act from where you are, that is all you can ever do. And, you can only act using the things you currently have at your disposal and from within your current environment.

So, you need to work out where you are, then you need to find out what you have, and then you must act from that place and by using those things. Many people, if not all, have an image in their mind of what they wish to have, do, or become, but the majority of people fail to make that first initial step because they feel they can only act when they get to a better place or when they have better things to use. Realise, that by taking that first step, you begin moving towards that better place. At the same time, the better place begins to move towards you and quite naturally, the better things to use will begin to present themselves. Buddha once said, "You don't need to see the whole staircase, you just have to take the first step". That is a psychological truth. By not acting, your situation stays the same, and you recycle the same experience over and over again. For a change of circumstance, you must take the first step of action and it's really important that you take it now, from where you stand, using what you have. Once you do that, the next step of the staircase will be presented to you.

So, to increase the efficiency of your action, there are just a few rules.

Firstly, you mustn't act with a divided mind, with your mind in the past or projected into the future. You must always act with your full energy directed and focused upon the present moment while holding your mind to the purpose of your vision. To act in any other way will decrease the efficiency of your action.

Secondly, you mustn't overwork yourself. Hard work doesn't get you that which you want, efficient work does. Success in any area of life is not the result of working tediously or the result of hard work. Success is the result of doing each and every separate act, as small as the act may be, in an efficient manner.

Thirdly, you mustn't rush. To rush is to compete. You are not a competitor, you are a creator and on the creative plane; there is plenty of time. Actions are better performed one by one, with your full attention on each given task, making sure that each specific part of each act is done in a perfect way. When it comes to actions, it is quality over quantity. One quality action transcends one hundred rushed actions. This isn't to say that you should act slowly, it means that you must never act in haste.

"The secret to getting ahead is getting started."

-Mark Twain

You now understand the four essentials. And your mind has been freed from the chains of fear, doubt, and worry. So, we are now set to conclude Part II and draw it to a close. We are ready to transition over to Part III where we will be making use of the knowledge we have learned thus far, by tying the knowledge to the maintenance of health.

PART III: APPLYING THE KNOWLEDGE TO THE ATTRACTION AND MAINTENANCE OF HEALTH

We are now ready to apply what we've learned, and we can now tie the knowledge to the maintenance of health. Remember, the knowledge is not limited to the maintenance of health, it can be applied to any area of your life including wealth, relationships, fame, or any other circumstance that you wish to experience. But for the purposes of this book, we will be concentrating on the area of maintaining health. So, let's get into it.

ENERGY FREQUENCY AND VIBRATION

Everything consists of energy, frequency, and vibration. To attract and maintain health, the goal is to get the energy that is your thoughts to vibrate to the frequency of health and keep it there. If all matter is merely energy condensed and vibrating to a frequency, it means that disease, being matter, is merely energy, condensed and vibrating to a frequency. If you zoom down to the subatomic level of an acorn, you will see that it is a vibrating string of energy. If you zoom to subatomic level into a sunflower seed, what you will see is that it, too, is a vibrating string of energy. They are identical at the subatomic level, yet they produce two completely different things when planted. Because within the energy, there is a specific vibratory pattern. An acorn vibrates to the frequency that produces the appearance of an acorn, whereas the sunflower seed vibrates to the frequency which produces the appearance of a sunflower seed. When an acorn is planted in the ground, its energy contains a vibratory pattern; one which dictates the frequency it emits. This frequency is what then attracts through the earth the energy which is in harmony to the frequency emitted by its vibratory pattern. Now think for a minute, imagine an oak tree. The oak tree has a completely different appearance to the acorn; an oak tree is not vibrating to the frequency of an acorn, for if it were, you would be looking at an acorn. The oak tree is vibrating to the frequency of an oak tree. Upon planting the acorn while abiding by its rules for growth, the acorn attracts to it the energy that is in harmony with itself; that is the energy of the potentiality of the oak tree. Once attracted, they merge as one and the roots begin to emerge and eventually, the oak tree makes its appearance. Energy cannot be created or destroyed; it can only transmute from one form into another. And so, the energy which merged with the acorn always existed. The frequency of the acorn brought the two together; it attracted to it the like energy and the two energies merged, resulting in the transmutation of an oak tree.

A lot of people fail to recognise the attraction of like energy, but the universe is riddled with examples of it. A good example is a sperm cell being attracted to an egg. The little guys don't have a brain or eyes to navigate. They are simply attracted to the egg because the vibratory pattern which makes up the sperm cell's energy is harmonious with the egg. Once it reaches the egg, the two merge and they transmute into a human being.

Now, in terms of disease in relation to a pandemic, disease will appear in the body of the one whose mind is favourable to its attraction. If the energy pattern of your thoughts is harmonious to the energy pattern of disease, the two will be attracted to one another—a virus or disease would be compelled to move towards you until it reaches you. When it reaches you, it will merge with your body and will appear in the form of disease. Likewise, health will maintain in the body if one's mind is favourable to it. The energy pattern of your thoughts will be harmonious with the vibratory pattern of health and so health will be compelled to move towards you. When it reaches you, it will merge with your body and it will appear in the form of health. Furthermore, the appearance of health shall remain, but only if the frequency of your thought's energy pattern doesn't waver from positive expectancy to negative expectancy. Like causes will always produce like effects.

THE MEDIA

To keep your thoughts vibrating to the frequency of health, you must turn off the media, or at the very least, you must learn to not be inundated by it. You must recognise the media as being the tool that it is; one which is designed to keep your thoughts vibrating to the frequency of fear and during a pandemic, disease. The media will keep you constantly thinking about the things in which you do not want to happen. Their main focus is to present to you the pessimistic side of life. This is achieved by presenting stories and propaganda which will instil negativity and misfortune in your mind. For this reason, when you are in the process of attracting and maintaining health, I highly recommend that you distance yourself from it completely. If, however, you feel that you must be informed, and would struggle to remove the media from your life completely, then a good first step is to only view the media with the knowledge of what it really is—a tool. To distract, misinform, programme, and instil fear in your mind. If you doubt this to be true, then I recommend that the next time you switch on the news, count how many negative suggestions are displayed in just a short 10-minute interval. Meanwhile, also count how many positive suggestions are displayed. You will see that the odds are largely in the favour of the negative suggestions.

If you are to watch the media, watch it with the intention of 'reading between the lines' because the media use language that can be likened to that of neuro-linguistic programming. And usually, whatever the media says, they usually mean the opposite. Regarding the coronavirus, they are using phrases designed to misinform. For example, instead of saying "10 people have died from coronavirus", they will instead use language such as "10 people have died after being tested positive for coronavirus". The difference is subtle, but it makes all the difference because the 10 people may not have actually died from the disease. The 10 people may have died from something else. All that the suggestion indicates is that upon their death, they had tested positive. This will cause the reader/viewer to presume that the disease had killed them when, in reality, they could have died from a natural cause or by some other underlying condition, whereby the fact they tested positive may have just been a mere coincidence.

So, if you do decide to watch it, watch it with awareness. Don't let it scare you, don't allow it to divert you from your goal of keeping your thoughts vibrating on a frequency of health. If you can, turn it off completely for having it on will do you no favours. Your health is your wealth. Being misinformed is sacrilege.

"If you don't read the newspaper, you're uninformed. If you do read the newspaper, you're misinformed."

-Mark Twain

THE COLLECTIVE CONSCIOUSNESS

When a pandemic strikes, due to the six basic human fears, the collective consciousness will be vibrating to the frequency of fear, doubt, and worry. Your job now is to pull away from the collective consciousness and not be a part of it. With the knowledge attained in Part I and II, you are equipped with the ability to pull out from the collective interconnected mindset. You have at your disposal working knowledge of your creative power, the universal laws, and have been introduced to the answers which nullify the six basic fears. This is sufficient enough to allow you to think with clarity and on your own terms, which will allow you to create and tune in to a reality of health. By adopting the philosophy contained herein and applying its principles as a matter of habit, you will remain in that reality.

Applied knowledge and faith will keep you safe. The collective consciousness is vibrating to a negative frequency during a pandemic, simply because the majority of individuals lack applied knowledge and faith. By having faith in your creative powers and by having faith in the universe, you will remove yourself from the collective which currently believes that the contraction of disease is down to external circumstance and mere chance or luck, which we know is not the case. Remember the quote from Buddha mentioned earlier in the book? "Every human being is the author of his own health and disease". He didn't say every human being is the author of his own health and disease except during pandemics. During a pandemic, there is no difference; it is you and you alone who will author your own state of health and it is you and you alone who can maintain it.

The collective consciousness is not a reliable friend at the best of times. In times like this, it is your enemy, so do not attach to it. Throughout history, humans have picked up a herd mentality simply because they are ruled by the six basic fears. The fear of criticism is the second most prevalent fear in the world, and it results in conformity. Conformity is a dangerous thing, especially when those that you choose to conform to are those who are simply conforming themselves. It is of no benefit for you to emulate those who are fearful in their thinking and who are lacking in an understanding of the true nature of their being and in their relationship to the universe.

As the old saying goes, "Birds of a feather will flock together", which basically means that people with similar tastes and interests stick together or form groups. Since 80% of the world is still operating from a low level of awareness, and since the system is designed in such a way that it encourages and focuses solely upon gossip and negativity, its result is that 80% of the world is vibrating to the frequency of fear, doubt, and worry. Due to this, they naturally flock together. Upon flocking together, outsiders are not welcomed. They are ridiculed for stepping out of line if they so ever dare present them with an idea which doesn't fit the beliefs of the collective consciousness.

Marconi was an inventor in the 1800s who, by using one of Nikola Tesla's patents, managed to transmit sound-waves wirelessly through the air. Upon revealing this discovery to the world, he was deemed mental and he was put in a straitjacket and shipped off to a mental hospital. Because, at the time, when there was no radio or anything of the like. It was a natural reaction to deem somebody who claimed that he could send voices wirelessly through the air from one location to another to be mentally unstable. Closed mindedness and ignorance derive from fear and a lack of awareness. And in this case, it caused a perfectly sane visionary to be locked in a psychiatric hospital. He was, however, later released after persuading one of the doctors to let him demonstrate his claims.

Cognitive dissonance is the opposing and rejecting of an idea without good cause simply because it contradicts one's own belief system. The majority of the world suffers from cognitive dissonance and the majority of the world tune in to the collective consciousness and abide by its confines. All for two reasons. Firstly, because they are not aware of how to transcend it and secondly, they tune into it as a survival mechanism. They are either simply not aware of anything beyond the level of awareness which the collective is vibrating or, simply, out of fear they feel the need to blend in and conform in hope that the 'herd' will protect them.

So, considering birds of a feather flock together, make sure you emulate the feathers of positivity—make sure that you flock to the right bird. The collective consciousness will be emitting the belief that you have no control over a pandemic, and it is crucial to your health that you pull away from that belief. Just because the majority of the world believes a lie, it doesn't mean that it becomes a truth. The power is within you and if you apply the principles outlined in this book, you can transcend your awareness beyond the confines of the collective consciousness.

"Two paths diverged in the woods, I took the path less travelled by, and that has made all the difference."

-Robert Frost

THE ANALOGY OF THE RADIO

To manifest health into your life, you must tune your thoughts into the frequency of health and align your thoughts up with that reality. Remember, the universe is infinite, so all potentialities and realities you could possibly imagine exists for you. There are an infinite number of health realities and there are an infinite number of disease realities. Your task is to turn the dial to a reality of health, which there are many. In fact, the odds are exactly 1:1 since infinity is whole—it cannot be divided against. So, it is just as easy to tune in to health as it is to tune in to disease. It is just a matter of how you set your sail of thought.

Our reality is very much like a radio that has infinite channels, and you can tune into any channel you want; you can choose to experience health, or you can choose to experience disease. Now, I assume you want to experience health, and if you already have health, then I assume you wish to maintain it. For the purpose of not leaving anything down to chance, you must learn to turn the dial consciously. If you desire health, you need to turn the dial of your mind and tune in to the reality of health. The turning of the dial is simple, the method by which you turn the dial and tune in to the reality of health can be summed up in three words: attention and expectation. The dial of your mind is attention and expectation because energy flows where attention goes, and the energy that flows will always behave how you subconsciously expect it to behave. The double-slit experiment gives plenty of credence to this.

You are free of fear, doubt, and worry as you have the knowledge to pull away from the collective consciousness. And now that the media isn't directing your energy of thought towards the energy of disease, you are now set to begin to attract and maintain health by turning the dial of your mind towards the energy of health by directing your attention towards it whilst simultaneously expecting to receive it.

"Man has been blessed with the control of just one thing. We can control what we think."

IT BEGINS WITH THOUGHT

To direct your attention towards the reality of health, thought is the starting point because thoughts are the result of attention. In guarding and observing your thoughts, you can calculate and control where your attention is focused. It is important that we are constantly thinking about being healthy. Thoughts of health provide feedback on where our focus is aimed and once you are focused on health, your thoughts will be aligned with the energy of health. Thoughts are what induce feelings. Thoughts set the energy in motion to attract and to bring to you the reality of health. By changing your thoughts to those of health, you will change your belief system to one that believes in health. This will, in turn, change how you perceive and how you feel. When this occurs, your actions will be based on that new belief system and off that new level of awareness. Your actions will be in alignment to the reception of health and they will, ultimately, be the cause of the habits you form. Your habits will attract the like effect that is a vibrational match to the root cause of the habit. The like effect will be the circumstance of health because the root cause of the habit was thoughts of health.

THE CONSCIOUS MIND

The conscious mind is the receiving station in the process of thought transmission. It receives impulses of thought through the sources of the five senses and infinite intelligence. To think thoughts of health, you must do two things. Firstly, you must conduct your environment in such a way that only the impressions of health reach your five senses and you must consciously reject any suggestions of disease which may arise as a result of your environment. Being the part of the mind, which chooses, and which thinks your conscious mind has the power to accept or reject any impression at will. Secondly, you must make sure that the impressions being received from infinite intelligence are impressions of health.

To conduct your environment in such a way is to shut out all ideas that do not resonate with the energy of health. These ideas are everywhere and can come in the form of other people's suggestions, media, social media, and TV. By paying attention to these suggestions, you are giving energy to them; you will internalise them and they will become a part of your belief system. And this is what we do not want to happen.

To ensure that the conscious mind only receives impressions of health from infinite intelligence, one must first ensure that the subconscious mind is only being fed—and accepting only—the impressions of health. The assurance of this will be drastically helped by the conducting of your environment as mentioned above. If you conduct your environment in such a way that your attention is only focused on the impression of health, and if you are able to consciously reject any impressions of disease, then the thoughts that you receive from infinite intelligence will ultimately be in alignment with the reality of health because no thoughts of disease are being handed over from your conscious to your subconscious mind.

Remember, the conscious mind is the cause of the effect. The effect is the manifestation. You want your manifestation to be a manifestation of health and so you need to make sure the cause is giving its attention to that which is favourable to the manifestation of health. By giving your attention to impressions of health, your conscious mind will cause its like effect; the like effect will be the effect which resonates to that which it gives its attention. The conscious mind does this by making use of the law, and the law is your subconscious mind.

THE SUBCONSCIOUS MIND

The subconscious mind is the sending station in the process of thought transmission. It accepts the impressions handed over to it from your conscious mind and sends the impression to infinite intelligence. Remember, the subconscious mind is subject to the will of the conscious mind and it will accept any thought handed over to it either by repetition emotionalization, expectation, or belief. The subconscious mind is very impressionable, so it is very important that you take control of your conscious mind for if you don't, unfavourable impressions will reach the subconscious mind, which will then proceed to translate that impression to infinite intelligence. We do not want thoughts of disease reaching infinite intelligence; we want only thoughts of health to make it there. Remember, the subconscious mind is the law. It doesn't choose, it doesn't think, it simply just acts on the material with which it is fed. So, it is your job to make sure your conscious mind is feeding the subconscious mind only the material which resonates with health. The two main ways to do this are through the use of creative visualisation and through the use of autosuggestion. When making use of these two methods of attracting health, it is extremely important that you begin making use of the four essentials. Refer back to Part II if necessary to re-familiarise yourself on how to intensify the four essentials.

CREATIVE VISUALISATION

Use creative visualisation to intensify the desire for health by giving it a purpose for its attainment, then keep this purpose fixed in your mind as you visualise. See yourself as a healthy individual and see yourself as doing all the things that a healthy individual does. Never permit any images related to disease to appear in your mind during the visualisation, for if you do, you will affect the potency of your image. The key to visualisation is detail. The effectiveness of this technique will depend largely upon how real you can make the visualisation feel. The subconscious mind cannot differentiate between a visualisation and real event. Therefore, if you make the visualisation as real as physically possible, the subconscious mind will act on the visualisation by accepting it as a matter of fact, which will cause it to seek to produce the image that was impressed upon it by externalising the intangible impression into a tangible actuality. Remember, the law obeys the cause. Your job is to get the cause to feel the experience of the visualisation so that the law will accept the visualisation as being real. This, in turn, will cause the law to generate its effect physically.

While you visualise, feel the positive feelings which arise as a result, and as you feel the positive feelings, express the attitude of gratitude and give thanks for the feelings. After giving thanks for the positive feelings, embody the emotion of faith and simply believe that health is yours and that health is being given to you. You then need to put in the efficient action necessary to align your actions with the actions contained within the thought that constitutes the image of health. In other words, harmonise your actions with the actions of the person with which you are visualising. Make these actions and the visualisation a habit. It isn't enough to merely set aside a special time during the day to visualise; you need to bring the visualisation to the point where it is fixed in your mind without effort on your part. If your desire is strong enough, the visualisation will fixate itself. Effort isn't required to keep your mind held to the image of a burning desire, for the burning desire will hold the image for you. However, if the attainment of the image isn't something that you really care about, some effort will be needed to keep the image fixed in your mind. You can remedy this by intensifying your desire, and by gaining a new purpose for its attainment.

Visualisation is prayer power, and the process of prayer power is mental verbalisation, picturization, and actualisation. If you mentally verbalise while you continuously picturise, you will consistently actualise. Prayer and visualisation are not something you do as a one-off throughout the day—your whole life should be a conscious prayer. The subconscious mind is susceptible to false and unfavourable impressions, and by drifting, you can allow these impressions to seep in. These unfavourable impressions lead to the experience of an unfavourable situation.

During a pandemic, it is easy to divert your attention towards disease and towards the symptoms of that disease. In doing so, you will create a corresponding picture of the disease and its symptoms in your mind, which is likely to induce negative feelings. These negative feelings, combined with the picture which they are attached to, will set the energy in motion to bring to you that disease and those symptoms. Keep your mind completely off the virus, don't think about it. Focus on what you do want—health.

Your mind should be consistently held to your vision. Your vision should be backed by faith and it should be powered by your purpose, and you must hold this purpose and vision with devout gratitude. If you do this, and if you never allow the image to fade, whatever it is that's held in the image will eventually seek outward physical expression. It will externalize itself and become your reality in the physical plane.

"The imagination is a preview of life's coming attractions."

-Albert Einstein

AUTOSUGGESTION

Use autosuggestion to consciously programme your subconscious mind. Throughout the book, you have been made aware of the immense power of suggestion and you can purposely use that power to keep yourself healthy during a pandemic. During a pandemic, suggestions of disease will be floating around everywhere; it is up to you to reject these suggestions and not allow them to make it past your conscious awareness and into your subconscious mind. Your inner dialogue with yourself can either be your best friend or worst enemy. Through autosuggestion, we repeat strings of commands to ourselves and when these commands are repeated often enough, and when they are emotionalized with either of positive or negative emotions, they are passed onto the subconscious mind where the thought will be translated into its spiritual equivalent and made manifest in the form of circumstance. During a pandemic, your goal is to keep your inner voice on the side of health and positive expectancy and away from disease and negative expectancy.

To use autosuggestion purposely, you must intentionally repeat strings of words which harmonise with your aim while, at the same time, stopping any negative suggestions in their tracks and rejecting them before they have time to take root. The ultimate goal is to tip the balance, even if it's just by 1%. It will be reassuring to know that one positive suggestion is worth ten negative suggestions and it's even more reassuring to know that you do not need to believe the suggestion at first. Through repetition, visualisation, and emotionalization, you can bring your subconscious mind to accept any thought that you desire to be accepted.

Use affirmations to programme your subconscious to the reality of health. Affirmations are a powerful tool if you emotionalize them with belief and repeat them. Eventually, they will be accepted as part of your subconscious beliefs and your subconscious beliefs are what dictates whether or not you will contract a disease or maintain health.

The affirmations in Part II are perfect for all areas of your life and they can literally transform your life if you use them correctly. To use affirmations correctly, you need to choose the ones which harmonise with your personal goals, or which represent who you wish to become. Use them during visualisation and tie them into the use of the four essentials. When using your affirmations, I recommend using them as often as practically possible. The most important time to affirm is directly upon arising in the morning and directly before going to sleep at night. During these two times, your brainwave activity is in an alpha wave state; alpha wave states are of a lower frequency and they dominate when the brain is relaxed. During this relaxed state, the subconscious mind is more susceptible to impressions because, with the conscious mind not fully alert, it drops its guard so to speak. So, any suggestion picked up by the conscious mind is more likely to seep into the subconscious mind. Not only this, the commands you give yourself just before sleep is acted upon throughout the night. During your sleep, your mind will work with the last thoughts given to it before drifting off. Likewise, in the morning when in an alpha brainwave state, the commands you give to yourself are what will set up your day. The alpha brainwave state is the state that is induced by meditation; it is the state that is induced by hypnotists on their subjects. A hypnotist purposely induces low-level brain activity to cause the conscious mind of the subject to lower its guard, with the aim of making the subjects subconscious mind more susceptible to his suggestions. So, during a pandemic, use these two times wisely and if you meditate, even better because then you can induce the state at will and it will serve you well when performing your visualisations and affirmations. I would further add that it is beneficial to repeat your affirmations one more time in the middle of the day just because it brings your mind back to where it needs to be in the likely case that it has drifted off throughout the course of the day.

Now, here are some health affirmations that can be repeated in times of disease, illness, pandemics, and whenever you generally feel like your vitality is beginning to sag. Repeat them aloud for maximum effect

Health affirmations

I am healthy   *I am well being*

I am robust   *I am strong*

I am vigorous   *I am vitality*

I am soundness   *I am healthiness*

I am salubrious   *I am healthful*

I am wholesome   *I am protected*

I am self-sustaining   *I am strengthening*

I am energetic   *I am intact*

I am flawless   *I am faultless*

I am unblemished   *I am clean*

I am purified   *I am safe*

THE METAPHYSICAL WAY

I am secure   *I am well*

I am depurated   *I am fitness*

I am in good condition   *I am in perfect health*

I am pure   *I am cleansed*

I am lively   *I am vibrant*

I am resilient   *I am preserved*

From these affirmations, you can make your own affirmations by moving them about and combining them. Just remember the rules for the connectors and the power words as mentioned in Part II.

I have added one below as an example. You would fare well to repeat the following affirmation at least three times a day, ideally morning, noon, and night. In light of a pandemic, it will serve as a prayer to yourself and keep you vital and secure.

"I am so happy that I am in perfect health. My body is strong, resilient, and preserved. My body is strengthening every day, and every day I feel more and more lively. I am safe, protected, and my loved ones are safe and protected, and for that, I am extremely grateful."

> "To think health when in the midst of disease requires power, but he who acquires that power becomes a mastermind. He can conquer fate; he can have what he wants."

> – Wallace D Wattles

BE WHAT YOU WANT TO ATTRACT

We don't attract that which we want, but rather that which we are. This is a simple statement but there is a simplicity in the statement that a lot of people seem to miss, and it seems to trip quite a lot of people up. You need to create the image of who you would like to be in your mind first, then you must live into that image; be sure to think and act in all the many ways that harmonise with the ways that the person in the image would think and act. Quite naturally before you know it, the image that was once in your mind will externalise itself. It will seek outward physical expression and you will, by emulating that image, literally become the image which you emulated. To earn the right to be the image that you imagine, you must do all the things that the person in the image would do. You must think, act, and be like that person. Before you know it, you will be. So, let us never forget; to become what you want to be, you must first be what you want to become.

"We don't attract the things we say we want, but that which we justly earn."

-Earl Nightingale

We are now drawing to a close on Part III and we'll be moving on over to Part IV where I will be providing some precautions, practicality, and a summary of Mind Over Microbes. In Part I and II, you received an abundance of essential knowledge. In Part III, we have tied that knowledge to methods that can be used as a defence in regard to the maintenance of health. But it doesn't stop there. You must internalise its principles until the understanding of them becomes second nature, and until you firmly believe what they say. It is up to you to use the techniques and make them work for you. I have written this book and kept it as short as physically possible in the hope that it will encourage a re-read and so that it can be used as a source of reference. I endeavoured to keep it short and to the point while at the same time, fitting in as much information as would be beneficial.

Let us conclude on Part III and transition over to Part IV

PART IV: PRECAUTIONS, PRACTICALITY, AND SUMMARY OF MIND OVER MICROBES

PRECAUTIONS

I now wish to provide you with a short list of precautions and suggestions.

o Question everything because that's the problem with people. People simply don't think for themselves. You have your own mind; you should never let another do your thinking for you because only you know what's best for yourself and only you should come to your own decisions. Don't believe everything you hear. Many people have parrot syndrome, whereby they repeat everything they hear without first checking to see if it's true. Learn to question all things. Even what was written in this book.

o Have an open mind at all times because a mind is like a parachute. It doesn't work if it's closed. The world is more mystical than it seems, so with an open mind, you will begin to notice that things aren't as they seem on the surface. And just when you think you've reached the bottom of the rabbit hole, it gets even deeper. With an open mind, life is a beautiful struggle. With a closed mind, it's just a struggle.

o Don't accept a 'mandatory' vaccine or an RFID chip. Accepting either of these won't do you any favours in the long run. Again, you have your own mind. It is just a suggestion, but one that I highly recommend you consider. I had to suggest this precaution simply for my own peace of mind.

PRACTICALITY

I will add some practicality here for the practically-minded. There is a three-part formula which has no equal when it comes to maintaining health by practical means. Nothing can compete with the health benefits gained by the combining of:

1) Positive thought
2) Deep breathing
3) Plenty of water

The combining of these three things, if adopted as a matter of habit, are the cornerstone to the practical aspect of a healthy life. Positive thoughts attract positive circumstances, deep breathing gives your brain adequate oxygen supply, and drinking plenty of water has an innumerable amount of health benefits.

If you do these three things, your body will remain healthy. Almost all disease occurs because of an insufficiency in either one or all of these three simple, essential habits. If you analyse the majority of people, you will quickly discover that a) they are always thinking negative, b) they have developed the habit of only taking half breaths, and c) they do not drink nearly half as much water as they should. It is of no surprise then that disease in modern society is so prevalent. If you remedy these three things and if you apply the principles outlined in this book, health will be compelled towards you. If you apply the philosophy herein and act on the three-part formula by adopting it as a matter of habit, health will not only be compelled towards you—it will be encouraged to stay.

Now, there are two more things that are important and can benefit your health astronomically. That is the type of food you eat and meditation.

Food

The food you eat plays an important role in your vibration, and your vibration is what dictates the frequency you're on. Low energy fatty foods, fast food, and a heavy meat-based diet will lower your vibrations. They say you are what you eat, and that saying has a lot more truth than most people realise because you are literally feeding off the vibration of that which you eat. I would recommend a vegetarian or a vegan diet personally, but that is just a suggestion, it is not essential. However, a vegetarian diet will key up the rate of vibration to such a point that it will allow you to attract and manifest with much greater ease. Heavy foods slow down the process, and they cause sluggish actions, but that is not to say that they hinder you completely. Fresh fruits and vegetables in the small quantities will charge you up like a battery and, thus, giving you more power to attract to you the circumstances of life which you wish to experience. By having control over what you choose to consume, you will also receive other benefits besides keeping you energised. Using the power of will in relation to food is not easy; unhealthy food is a tempting gluttonous pleasure and so the ability to refrain from the temptation provides you with discipline. He who can control the food that he consumes can control everything else. A healthy mind will express itself through a healthy body; if one makes his thoughts healthy, he will no longer desire unhealthy food. And that is a statement of truth.

Meditation

Meditation and its amazing health benefits cannot be emphasised enough. You don't need to shave your head, put on a robe, or completely rearrange your life and become a monk. Meditation is simply a therapeutic agent, and with the exception of the act of sex perhaps, it is a therapeutic agent that has no equal. Meditation can be used for visualisation, working on the four essentials, and the removal of negative emotions. The act of meditation will bring your brain wave activity to that which is akin to the level of activity just prior to sleep. In this relaxed state, you can ask for guidance from infinite intelligence and you will most certainly receive it because meditation will enhance the power of your intuition which, in turn, will increase the receptiveness of your creative imagination. In this relaxed state, any temporary worries will cease to exist. From here, you can go deeper into who you are, where you want to go, and from here, you can request replenishment and bring your body to a healthy state.

SUMMARY OF MIND OVER MICROBES

The universe consists of swarms of energy that are vibrating to a particular frequency. Your thoughts are energy and they, too, vibrate to a particular frequency. With the universe being infinite, there are an infinite number of realities that exist for you, and by using the mental faculties of the mind, you can consciously tune in to the reality which you wish to experience. To tune into the reality you want, you must pull away from the collective consciousness and you must learn how to turn the dial of your mind. The turning of the dial can be summed up in three words: attention and expectation. You need to focus your attention on exactly what it is that you want to experience and meanwhile, you must expect that the thing which you want is being given to you. To do this, you must first master the four essentials: desire, faith, gratitude, and efficient action. Once mastered, you then must adopt the four essentials and apply them as a matter of habit. Once adopted, you must form the mental picture of the things you wish to have, do, or become, and you must hold this picture with unwavering consistency as you back it with faith and power it with purpose. All the while, you must express an attitude of gratitude. To do this, use creative visualisation and fix your efforts upon the visualisation until the visualisation fixates itself.

Be sure to remember what you really are, understand why it is you are here, and never permit yourself to forget where it is that you came from or where it is that you are going. By understanding the answers to these questions, you will keep fears, doubts, and worries at bay, which will ultimately allow you to make positive use of the four essentials when attempting to make use of the mental faculties. Stay clear of any negative outside influences and negative suggestions. If you can, turn off the media, and don't engage in any conversation which doesn't harmonise with your vision for health and success. Use affirmations to programme your subconscious mind to more desirable pursuits. Affirm immediately upon arising in the morning and prior to going to sleep at night. And, as you affirm, see the words as being true and be thankful for the reality of them. Don't forget; the three-part formula: positive thoughts, deep breathing, and plenty of water. Try your best to remind yourself to do these three things every day until they form as a matter of habit. Watch what food you eat, cut down on low energy foods where you can and substitute them for high vibrational foods such as fruits and vegetables. Practice meditation; meditation is a useful tool that will keep you vital, free of worry, and it can sharpen your intuition and keep your mind on the right track. Stay positive. Like causes always produce like effects, a positive mind will bring you positive results and it can be no other way. The universe operates according to law and order—it never does, and it never can operate by disorder or chance.

Existence is much more mystical than we think it is, to the extent that I just could not explain. And it's by the very act of digging into it that you soon come to the realisation that you quite simply don't have a big enough shovel. Infinity cannot be comprehended, and so, I don't believe that it's our job to try. Our job is to simply express it; that's all we can ever do.

But there is one thing that I do know for sure, and it's that there is more to you than meets the eye. You see, the truth is… you are not just an extension of the universe, for the universe is also an extension of you. You are not just the thought of the whole, you are also the expression of that thought. You are literally both the cause and the effect of existence. You are pure consciousness, and consciousness is infinite; infinity is boundless and so this is why you really can have, do, or be anything you want.

"Existence, it's just a thought. We are simply expressions of that thought.

We are energy, in motion, flowing with the rhythm of life.

We are dancing, to one tune, the tune of God.

To just one song. And that's why we call it the universe."

-T.D.C Schofield

THE END

Made in the USA
Monee, IL
23 June 2020